This lucid, scholarly and readable book aims to help tl
his horoscope – or that of another person – by tl
Chinese method. Beginning with the date and hour of birth and using the methods of Chinese divination it is possible to discover the four pillars that rule our destiny.

The Chinese have many methods of divination, none of which can truly be termed astrology. The whole subject of divination is covered in the first part of this book, which also explains the Chinese calendar and its importance. The second half of the book is concerned with practicalities – a method of working out a horoscope and interpreting it.

Jean-Michel de Kermadec lived and worked in China for many years and his extensive knowledge of China, its culture, traditions and peoples is expressed in this book. As John Blofeld writes in his foreword, 'the names of most of the chapters read like a catalogue of matters having more or less bearing on almost every field of Chinese study. Never to my knowledge have these matters as a whole been so lucidly set forth in either French or English'.

Derek Poulsen was born in North China. In 1948 he qualified as a British Army interpreter in Chinese in Peking. Later he was a member of the Chinese and Burmese sections of the BBC External Services.

The Way to Chinese Astrology

The Four Pillars of Destiny

JEAN-MICHEL HUON DE KERMADEC

Translated by
N. Derek Poulsen

Foreword by
John Blofeld

London
UNWIN PAPERBACKS
Boston Sydney

First published in Great Britain by Unwin Paperbacks 1983

UNWIN® PAPERBACKS
40 Museum Street, London WC1A 1LU, UK

Unwin Paperbacks,
Park Lane, Hemel Hempstead, Herts HP2 4TE

George Allen & Unwin Australia Pty Ltd.,
8 Napier Street, North Sydney, NSW 2060, Australia

British Library Cataloguing in Publication Data

Poulsen, Derek
The way to Chinese astrology.
1. Astrology, Chinese
I. Title
133.5′0951 BF1714.C5

ISBN 0–04–133010–2

Set in 11 on 13 point Times by
Nene Phototypesetters Ltd, Northampton
Printed in Hong Kong by
Dah Hua Printing Press Co. Ltd.

TO
MY BELOVED
YANRU

My Chinese Eyes

饮水思源

'If you drink water,
remember the spring'

Most of the illustrations in this book were first published in the French edition: *Les Huit Signes de votre Destin* (L'Asiathèque, Paris) and are reproduced by arrangement with them. The cover illustration is by Louis Constantin, with Chinese calligraphy on the cover and on the dedication page by HSIUNG Ping-ming. Ideograms throughout the book are by LAN Yanru.

ACKNOWLEDGEMENT

When at the end of 1978 I asked my old friend Derek Poulsen to help me with the translation of a book I was going to publish in French on Chinese divination, *Les Huit Signes de votre Destin*, I could not foresee the tremendous amount of work we would have to grapple with. Derek Poulsen is like myself an old China Hand, so our team was well matched. He is also a perfectionist, and it was soon apparent that a mere translation would be inadequate. We found that the French way of thinking was both too logical and too conceptual. We had to rewrite and reconstruct the entire book to make it comprehensible and accessible to an English reading public. If a reader compares the English and French versions they will soon see what is meant.

On one of the many occasions when I visited Canterbury to work on the book with Derek Poulsen I met John Blofeld, whom we had both known long ago in Peking. His warm approval of the book was most welcome. He helped us to find a publisher and wrote the brilliant essay which constitutes the Foreword. He has our deepest gratitude.

Canterbury, September 1982

Publisher's Note

SEASONAL INFLUENCES IN THE SOUTHERN HEMISPHERE

The ancient Chinese knew nothing of the Southern Hemisphere and took no account of it in their astrological calculations. This is not so serious a matter as it may seem at first sight as Winter and Summer are composed of similar patterns of Yin and Yang. A person born in the Southern Hemisphere needs only to read Winter for Summer, Spring for Autumn, or vice versa, when assessing the influence of the seasons on their horoscope. It is important to remember that the Chinese seasons commence one and a half months before the comparative seasons of the Western calendar.

FOREWORD

The author of this book, having honoured me with an invitation to write a foreword, has taken the wind out of my sails by saying lucidly in the first three chapters almost exactly what I would otherwise have written! So what remains? I am inclined to think that some of my thoughts may add something of value to the book itself by setting this Chinese system of divination in a wider context, although at the cost of seeming sometimes to depart from the subject in hand to an almost inexcusable extent.

A difficulty likely to be experienced by some readers is that the system of divination and the underlying philosophy set forth here are the products of a way of thinking that differs markedly from all the modes of thought familiar to the peoples of the West. In the last century, when Western research into Eastern teachings first began – and for long after that – most people found it hard to take seriously beliefs having no accordance with their own. Chinese or, say, ancient Egyptian beliefs might be deemed quaint, picturesque, amusing or even comparatively wise, but even in this last case the assumption was that such wisdom was of a lower order than our own. Whereas a Western scholar who believed in palmistry or astrology might be deemed no worse than mildly eccentric, one who set store by the Chinese system in this book would surely have been thought crazy.

Indeed, as late as 1933, a senior English officer in the Hongkong government solemnly assured me that people who study Chinese are likely to go mad! That was at one time a widely held belief in England. Much more surprising to me, and even wounding, was the news that the famous Chinese scholar, Arthur Waley, was in the late 1950s only just dissuaded by a mutual friend from advising a publisher not to accept my translation of a famous book of divination, the *I Ching*, on the grounds that 'John Blofeld must be off his head – he seems to believe that *I Ching* predictions really work!'

However, by that time (as a result of closer contacts between East and West during and after World War II) Western opinion regarding such matters had generally advanced. Today, outstanding scholars like Arnold Toynbee and Joseph Needham (following Einstein before them, although his view of Eastern wisdom may not be generally known) have come to recognise that Chinese, Buddhist and other schools of Eastern thought have made or can make great contributions to the sum of human knowledge. That is not to say that any of the scholars just mentioned would go so far as to accept a Chinese method of divination as valid; for scholars with a Western background are naturally and rightly conservative in their approach. Therefore, however open-minded, they do not easily accept the validity of Eastern teachings that come into conflict with Western scientific notions. Uncritical acceptance is common enough now, but not among trained scholars.

Now, much as I applaud the scholarly approach and prefer it to a current tendency to rush into the acceptance of Eastern beliefs for emotional rather than intellectual reasons, I am convinced that Western scholars, and all the millions of modern Asians who tend to side with them, labour under a disability that sets limits on their understanding. As the heirs of Aristotle, Newton, Darwin and their modern successors, their thinking does in fact rest upon certain seldom varying assumptions, even though these may not necessarily be consciously entertained. For certain military and economic reasons, modern science remained for so long almost a monopoly of the West as to make some of its basic assumptions appear to shine with the light of Eternal Truth. This has tended to exclude from serious scientific enquiry, at least until quite recently, much that requires belief in supernatural agencies, or bears that appearance.

It so happened that, at the age of twenty with education incomplete and mind as yet unformed, I went to China. There, without any reservations whatsoever, I set myself to studying the beliefs of the ancient peoples (Chinese, Tibetan, etc.) of that region, supposing that much of what has managed to survive among them for upwards of a thousand years (in some cases perhaps five thousand) must surely have intrinsic merit. Even if some of the manifestations of Chinese belief crossed the borders of what used to be called the supernatural, that did not deter me. I was prepared to accept whatever strange teachings were offered, provided that they continued over a period of several years not to outrage my arbitrary but malleable convictions as to what is and is not possible. Needless to say, during the course of those years, I encountered a certain amount of nonsense, but also marvellous wisdom.

What I presently discovered was that very few traditional Chinese assumptions fitted well with what I had been taught to revere in my boyhood days. Specifically, I came across whole systems of belief that can be subsumed in the category, NOT TWO. That is to say, such dualisms as creator and created, mind and body, spirit and matter, mind and matter, subject and object, I and other were entirely foreign to my Chinese and Tibetan teachers' modes of perception. Indeed, they were persuaded that every kind of dualistic thinking is a product of gross ignorance! I remembered that Christian missionaries had for a century or more castigated the Chinese as 'gross materialists', on the ground that the popular Chinese concept of heaven very closely resembled the Chinese Empire, with its hierarchy of officials, underlings and servants. What the missionaries had overlooked or dared not say was that the Chinese concept of heaven as a close counterpart of earth could equally be the product of 'gross materialism' or of the notion that all things, above and below, are manifestations of spirit, there being no ultimate distinction between spirit and matter.

In this I found a valuable key to approximate understanding of the Chinese view of the universe, which is often expressed in a manner reminiscent of a dictum of the astronomer, James Jeans, to the effect that the stuff of the universe may well prove to be 'mind-stuff'.

Anyway, as a result of my 'openness' to whatever my Chinese teachers chose to tell me, I came at last to experience what traditionally minded Westerners might suppose to be a delusion, namely that one can experience modes of perception entirely beyond the range of what we have been taught to regard as normal. Furthermore, this type of perception brings with it a conviction of having come much closer than before to direct perception of Ultimate Truth: Reality! One knows soberly and positively that no delusion is involved; but, unfortunately, in seeking to prove this to other people, he encounters a problem similar to that of having to prove that cherries are redder than apples to a person born colour-blind. Only those who have themselves experienced that perception will know whether or not he is telling the truth. One fruit of that perception is direct understanding of what is meant by saying that the entire universe is composed of a single substance or non-substance that can best be described as 'mind-stuff' or just 'mind'.

Appreciation of the non-dual nature of ourselves and the universe in which we live brings one much closer to understanding the principles underlying this book of divination. Fortunately, however, the system taught in the book can be used effectively even without that understanding. In such a case, however, its effectiveness can be demonstrated only by the results achieved.

The first three chapters of this book contain, at least in essence, the fundamental concepts that have underlain, without much radical change, the whole vast realm of traditional Chinese religion, philosophy, art, government, education and way of being over a period of several thousand years. Is it really possible that a marvellously profound civilisation with prodigiously extensive and varied categories of achievement can have arisen from principles simple enough – that is simple *in a way* – to be conveyed to a reader in less than twenty pages? With any other civilisation, even one of narrow limits and no great depth, that would probably be beyond the scope of human ingenuity; whereas, with China, it *is* possible and has been done in those opening chapters. How so? Because the Chinese see (or used until recently to see) the universe and every single one of its innumerable aspects as conforming to a wonderful but quite uncomplicated pattern which, though capable of an infinite variety of detail, never departs from its primal essence. At the heart of things, in their middle and throughout every atom within their circumference, there is One. It has no shape, form, colour, texture, smell, sound or any definable characteristic whatsoever, and is yet endowed with the potentiality of creating from its own non-substance absolutely everything that is in existence or capable of being imagined. Formless, it cannot be known or directly perceived and it is therefore indescribable. Arbitrarily, it has been named Tao – the Way; but if you like to call it God, Reality, or any other name it will be neither more nor less appropriate.

What is formless must in itself be unchanging, there being nothing in illimitable void to undergo change, yet it functions through unceasing change of limitless variety. The changes are wrought by the emergence from the Tao of polarities named Yin and Yang, the one static and negative, the other dynamic and positive. Between them they comprehend the entire range of polarities. Note that they are by no means opposites; neither could exist in isolation from the other, since to be this but not that would require separation from the Tao, which is simultaneously everything. Partners in the dance of life, they merge in endless combinations from which all the fleeting, so-called entities comprising the universe are born. In short, everything partakes of the nature of everything else. However complex the activities of each may be, fundamentally they and all their functions are identical in nature. Therefore, an overall pattern can be deduced which can serve, among many, many other things, as a guide to a wise, wholesome and happy existence: that is what this book, based on a somewhat more intricate pattern derived from the primal pattern, provides.

Certain other works reflecting the wisdom of Taoist sages are so worded that they can be read at different levels according to need: as a guide to classical Chinese war strategy; as an alchemic treatise setting forth the means of converting base metals into gold; as a manual of sexual practice aimed at the attainment of vigorous health, longevity, strength, joy and virtue; as a textbook of instruction as to how the mystical experience of fusion between the individual mind and the totality of the cosmos can be attained; and so on. These widely disparate matters are not dealt with one by one consecutively. Each sentence can be read as simultaneously applying to each and all. This is entirely possible because knowledge of the underlying pattern can be applied to every form of human activity.

The present work has a more limited, but nevertheless valuable, aim. By a system evolved from the primal Yin Yang pattern, and in close accord with it, the book enables each individual user to make the best of the situation governing his personal existence. Human life, however enjoyable at times, is of course inseparable from such painful experiences as giving birth, illness, the disabilities of old age, death, bereavement, disappointment, loss and so on. Their intensity, frequency and painfulness can in many cases be minimised by people with knowledge of the workings of the Tao and of the flow of entities derived from them. Knowledge of factors most likely to affect us directly can be obtained from this book. With its help, though none of us can change our destiny, we can ameliorate many of its effects. Joys can be enhanced, some sorrows avoided and some other sorrows made more bearable.

The workings of the Tao by means of the interplay of Yin and Yang are never rigid, but indeed so flexible that there is a good deal of leeway for the operation of personal choice. Though the primal system, *taken as a whole*, never ceases to maintain an exquisite harmony, its constituent parts (such as individual people) experience a considerable degree of random chance. The use we make of free will, within the sometimes broad and sometimes narrow sphere at our disposal, is what largely determines the extent of happiness we enjoy in life. Therefore there is need for reliable guidance. A book of divination, derived from a detailed pattern (such as the 60-year, 60-day, 60-hour cycles, the twelve animal symbols and so on) that is correctly related to the primal pattern, can, of course, assist in making wise choices. A harmonious life is attainable only by avoidance of excess and every other kind of extreme. That is obvious; but, without guidance, we may be involved in extremes that we could not foresee.

Since the harmony of the whole universe does not depend on its infinitesimal individual parts being identical, we all differ from one another. One of the saddest differences is that the scope for attaining a big share of the good things of life varies among individuals to an extent that appears exceedingly unjust. Whether this is due to *karma*, God or fate is no part of my present theme; in any case the fact remains that individual scope for exercising free will varies enormously. Well, no system of divination can help someone to leap beyond the boundaries limiting the extent of free choice, whether these are narrow or far-flung. Nevertheless, such a book as this one, wisely used, can certainly make his situation much more tolerable.

That there are indeed certain universal patterns, as widespread as the one on which this book is based, is apparent on every hand. One has only to reflect upon the extraordinary likenesses found among disparate forms of nature to recognise that universal patterns are no myth. Take, for example, those small shells and plants found at the bottom of the ocean and consider the astonishing similarity of their patterns to those formed by lofty mountains and great trees on land. A more typically Chinese example is to be found in the grain of the Tali marble that comes from Yunnan province. The likeness of this grain to the black and white landscape paintings of Chinese artists is remarkable. Confronted by photographs of slabs of Tali marble and of typical Chinese landscape paintings, one may sometimes have difficulty in discovering which are which. If one accepts the existence of universal patterns (of which, however, the components are rarely identical in detail) and reflects that the pattern on which this book is based has been accepted by the Chinese as valid for thousands of years, it will not be difficult to put faith in that validity and act accordingly – as, indeed, the Japanese, Koreans, Vietnamese, Tibetans, Mongols and, to a lesser extent, the Laos, Thais and Cambodians have long been doing.

This book should also be of particular interest to a fair number of people not especially interested in divination; for the names of most of the chapters read like a catalogue of matters having more or less bearing on almost every field of Chinese study. Never to my knowledge have these matters as a whole been so lucidly set forth in either French or English. For me personally, the book will remain a valuable reference work, whether or not I am tempted to use it for divination.

JOHN BLOFELD
January, 1982

CONTENTS

Introduction

There are those who do not believe in astrology and there are others who assert that it is a science. Following the doctrine of the *Golden Mean*, dear to the Sages of China, I am inclined to disregard such extreme points of view.

Those who wish to reduce the admirable faculties of man to reasoning alone depress me. It is as frustrating to talk to them as it would be to discuss the colours of the rainbow with a man born blind. I suggest that they should consider the example of doctors still practising traditional medicine in China who, though conditioned by Marxist rationalism, nevertheless continue peacefully to employ a system of acupuncture which is based on thousands of years of empiricism, but for which to this day no rational explanation has been given. Chinese divination cannot properly be called a science, if science is a logical construction of the mind.

But if, beyond the limits of your reason, you believe that intuition and poetic inspiration can transform your view of the world, read on. In doing so – and this is my theme – you will, I hope, gain a new insight into yourself and others. Should you believe or not believe in astrology? In my view this question makes no sense and requires no reply: study the eight signs, which make up the Four Pillars of your destiny and you will see.

It seems necessary to make two points to help you to understand better the spirit in which a Chinese approaches the art of the horoscope.

The first is that no astral theme is definitive: it is merely a diagnosis. No serious astrologer believes that his analyses or predictions are binding, for he is aware of the old adage *astra inclinant non necessitant* – the stars predispose, they do not constrain. The Chinese would certainly agree with it if they thought it useful to formulate a truth which in their eyes is quite obvious: our fate is never completely settled.

We are not left without defence against blind fate or the forces loosed against us. To understand our destiny and the forces which dominate it helps us to turn it to better account and as far as possible to avoid its snares. The establishment of a horoscope thus has an eminently moral purpose. Besides, the Chinese have too much good sense not to take account of the relative importance of individual lives and too strong a sense of humour to take things tragically. Wisdom consists of laughing at oneself, in trying to take better advantage of that which is granted to us. Sometimes it will be necessary to swim with the tide; at others to swim or to row (to use a more Chinese image) against it. As with our health, for better or worse we have to accept our character and our destiny. In either case, to know ourselves is a help.

A second point which is easier to put into words than it is to put into practice, is that it is necessary to avoid thinking of this kind of horoscope as an identity photograph which gives a static image of your personality. One frame of a cinematic film has no life because there is no movement. The tragedy of the Western system of knowledge is that to analyse time it is necessary to stop it and then cut it out and thus deny it. It is the paradox of Western science which tries to discover the secret of life by dissecting corpses! Any static image is only one view of the mind. In setting their faces against metaphysics, the Chinese are perhaps better philosophers than we in the West. They have never thought of time and space as separate entities and have thus, unlike us, avoided the sophistries of Zeno of Elea.

Throughout this work we shall see that for the Chinese everything, even writing, is essentially dynamic and in movement. The horoscope will not discover for us the elements of a compound but rather the forces of action and interaction which are indissolubly tied to all the energies of the Universe. It is only when we come to know them that our free will is able to make use of these forces and to turn them to the best advantage.

For a Chinese the eight signs which determine his destiny are charged with meaning and should be considered with respect. Like all written ideograms, each of them is a gesture written visibly in space and which must be repeated in order to be understood. They constitute a means of entering into a relationship with the forces which rule us.

It was my good fortune that I was able to live for many years in an entirely Chinese environment and even greater good luck to have married a Chinese lady from Peking. My love for her was the third eye which helped me to penetrate this seductive universe, which was at the same time extremely disconcerting. An adequate knowledge of the Chinese language was the first indispensable key and friendship was the other.

This experience enabled me to establish that the Chinese, though little inclined to excessive religiosity in their daily lives, were nevertheless concerned to discover what destiny might have in store for them: whether, by consulting the calendar, they tried to determine the most favourable time to carry out some important undertaking, or whether, by establishing their horoscope, they attempted to divine the influences which ruled their family and social relations. In this way I was led to realise the importance in their eyes of the eight signs which allowed them to draw up their horoscope and define their personality.

In social relations, even in matters of business, one often hears in China the question: 'Under what cyclic animal were you born?' The question is asked not from curiosity about your age, but because the answer gives a first assessment of the chances for understanding and of the quality of the relationship it is hoped to establish. Although, in this case, the concern is with years and not months, the approach is analogous to that of those who, for example, are investigating the chances of an Aries and a Cancer arriving at a friendly or a loving relationship.

For day to day relationships, it is enough to know that particular one of the eight signs with which your cyclic animal is associated. But if one envisages a more lasting relationship or even marriage, it would be wise to consult all eight signs. In some cases, however, this knowledge and that of your personal name could become dangerous in the hands of ill-intentioned persons. I cannot help thinking that it is not a matter of chance that Mao Tse-tung's exact date of birth has never been revealed.

I am passionately interested in everything which concerns Chinese customs and the Chinese mentality; and it was with amused curiosity that I set myself to study the eight signs of destiny. Sceptical at first, I was encouraged by the results and my interest being caught I began to assemble the elements of this work. The purpose of this book is to help the reader cast his horoscope – or that of another person – by the traditional Chinese method. To do so it is first necessary to establish his astrological theme, combined with the necessary intuition and lucidity to interpret it. Beginning with his date and hour of birth he must, like a Chinese calendarist whose method is quite different from ours, discover the eight signs which rule his destiny. In China, time is defined by two series of cyclic characters, one of ten and the other of twelve, which, grouped two by two, rule respectively the year, the month, the day and the hour. In popular tradition, the twelve character series is more closely associated with a list of twelve animals and is used principally to name years.

All this will be made clear in the second part of the book which, for the benefit of the reader interested mainly in practicalities, is devoted to the method of working out a horoscope and then how to interpret it.

Clearly, in a work of this kind, the explanation of the methods used, though comprehensive, must be kept as simple as possible. Nevertheless, the reader will find that with application he will achieve an expertise which will enable him to detect new facets in the interpretation of character and temperament.

An astrological theme should be assessed as objectively as possible, without taking into account any personal knowledge of the person concerned. Indeed it is much easier to avoid all prejudice by working on the horoscope of someone who is quite unknown. Then when you do meet him, human contact helps to clarify his theme.

It is also necessary to remember that the horoscope indicates only the potentialities of a subject in much the same way as a hand in a game of cards. Influences of environment, of parents and relations and of events can modify or even destroy tendencies and change the behaviour of an individual.

The Chinese have many methods of divination, none of which can truly be called astrology. The stars may form the basis of calculations of the calendar; the months may be based on the revolutions of the moon and the twenty-eight zodiacal constellations of the lunar dwellings may dominate the days, but the eight signs are really numbers and Chinese divination (this applies to the *I Ching*[1] as well) should more accurately be described as numerology.

In the first part of this book, I cover the whole subject in a scientific way and try to make clear the Chinese concept of divination and to explain their calendar and its importance in their eyes.

My sources have been above all my many Chinese friends, not forgetting the second-hand booksellers with whom I loved to pass the time of day and from whom I obtained the essential documentation for this work: popular almanacs and innumerable booklets of divination. Naturally I was speedily obliged to have recourse to classical works, notably the most venerable of them, the *I Ching*, the Book of Changes, as well as to the relevant chapters *(Yüeh Ling)* which discuss the calendar in the *Li Chi*, the Book of Rites. At the same time I made careful study of chapters 66, 67, 68 and 74 in the oldest book of Chinese medicine, the *Nei Ching*, which contains the conversations between the legendary Emperor Huang Ti and his wise counsellor. These chapters give a comprehensive view of the connections which exist between the cyclic characters, the Five Agents, the points of the compass, bodily organs, colours, etc. . . .[1]

With the exception of R. P. Havret and Joseph Needham,[2] sinologues have been of little help to me. My subject would undoubtedly seem to them hardly worthy of their consideration, but above all my attitude is the reverse of theirs. They cannot resist using Chinese concepts to build philosophical constructions which conform with Western rationalism and which, unhappily, are seldom in touch with Chinese reality.

Similarly I have in my possession ten quite different translations of the *Tao Te Ching*, 'Book of the Way and its Virtue', the celebrated work of Lao Tzŭ, the father of Taoism. In the preface to his work and to justify its utility, each translator begins modestly by anathemising all the others in declaring himself the sole bearer of the authentic tradition. I prefer myself to rely on the old sage's text, of which the first line is a precise warning against the temptation to philosophise.[3]

I have also deliberately refrained from transposing Chinese divination into Western concepts, but on the contrary have sought to accustom you to look at it as the Chinese do. If in doing so, I am able to draw back for you only a corner of the atavistic veil of incomprehension which, according to Kipling, must necessarily separate East from West, it will be no small thing.

My chief personal contribution to this work has been to elaborate a practical method for a Westerner to find his eight signs with ease and without having to undertake the difficult task of studying the calendar.

Among the innumerable interpretations of the signs I have obviously looked for those which seemed the best, but above all those which could be understood by Western readers without, I hope, suppressing their exotic flavour.

It must now be obvious that I am presenting a personal version of my Chinese experience and that I have forced myself to set down as faithfully as possible the message which I have received. At the same time I am fully aware, in an age of radio and television, that, in the transmission of a broadcast, the quality depends in great part on the receiver through which you hear it.

Part I

MAN AND THE WAY

The White Tiger, symbol of the West and of the *Yin* principle, carrying the Five Agents: on the head Fire, doubled after the principles of cosmic astrology; on the right paw Wood; on the left Earth; on the thigh Metal, and at the end of the tail Water. Wood engraving taken from a popular manual of divination.

Chapter 1

The Chinese Vision of the World
The *Tao* and its Virtue

MAN IN THE UNIVERSE

It is almost a commonplace to say that the Chinese lack a 'metaphysical bump' and that they distrust instinctively explanations that are too rational. Confucius is a perfect interpreter of his countrymen when he blandly answered a question of one of his disciples with the words: 'I know nothing of man; how can I speculate on the nature of spirits?'[4] To vain speculations the Chinese will always prefer wisdom based on ancient experience which aims only at getting the best possible out of our human condition.

The Chinese are a nation of peasants attached to the land and their conception of the world is fashioned by the nature of the soil, the climate, the advantages and the constraints imposed on them by the region they inhabit. Like all good peasants, they have the tenacity and the realism of those who know that their survival depends more than anything else on their courage and labour. They are also aware that they are dependent on forces which they do not control, but which it is necessary for them to know if they are to profit by them or to alleviate their disadvantages.

Regular seasonal changes and the succession of day and night suggest to them the idea of a natural and beneficient order to which it is important to conform: if there are to be prosperous harvests, it were better to take account of the seasons and follow a calendar.

Nevertheless, in the midst of this natural order which is more regular in China than elsewhere, cataclysms which are unforeseen and often inexplicable make themselves felt. For the Chinese this disorder is the Evil and it comes from excess or imbalance in favour of an element which is not, however, evil in itself: neither aridity of the soil induced by an excess of drought nor floods from an excess of humidity are in themselves harmful; it is their exclusive predominance which is evil. Balance is necessary, therefore, for the maintenance of order. We shall see elsewhere that equilibrium itself should not be excessive, for that would lead to stagnation. The Chinese are fundamentally opposed by character and tradition to the Manichean dichotomy which opposes Good to Evil. For them nothing is evil in itself. Excess alone is a fault. Defying extremes, wisdom consists in maintaining the *Golden Mean*, so dear to Confucius.[5]

The evidence that it is necessary to conform to the laws of nature in order to survive, and the intuition that man, placed between Heaven and Earth, is a microcosm analogous to the macrocosm of the Universe, to whose laws he submits, leads to the belief that this unlawful disorder was in a sense a reaction of the Universe when man transgressed its laws. In this context, chastisement is thus seen less as the correction or punishment of the guilty, but rather as a necessary reparation for the re-establishment of the order on which depends the prosperity of all.

The order from on High, which shapes and determines order on earth, is thus the supreme law of human behaviour written in this universe. To understand this order the better to conform to it is the wisdom which leads to prosperity and that supreme equilibrium called

Harmony by the Chinese, while to misunderstand it can lead only to misery and suffering. The role of the Emperor, the 'Son of Heaven', consisted essentially in putting the Universe, expressively described as 'that which is under Heaven', in harmony with the celestial order; and the understanding of this celestial order, which permitted order and prosperity in the Empire, was the first duty of the Emperor and for which he was invested with the 'Mandate of Heaven'.

All this helps one to understand without further emphasis that the Chinese peasant has not tried to define a cosmogony which provides a rational explanation of the world. He wants only to determine those rules of practical morality which will allow him to assure his survival and to better the conditions of his existence. He is concerned with finding a practical morality in his search for Good, in other words, that which is useful in human life. He is not concerned with trying to discover Truth, a quest which would be not only useless but impossible. With Pilate he would willingly say: 'What is Truth!' Further, this morality is not based on a search for individual salvation in another world; it aims above all at bettering the everyday condition of life of man in society. The Taoists themselves have never tried to build philosophic structures but solely, in the light of reason, to realise an experience of intuition which is both mystical and poetic. If it is vain and foolish to discuss the nature of things in a scholarly fashion with Lucretius, our reason is perfectly capable, in its own domain, of profiting from experience and making better use of the world which surrounds us. Aristotle's vision of the celestial spheres was false, but his calculations gave a precise enough calendar and, what is more important, permitted the organisation of time. It is always permissible to abandon an hypothesis of work if a better one allows us to improve our hold on the Universe. The Chinese would not have condemned Galileo before knowing if his theories improved astronomy. But they would have thought him a dangerous dreamer if he had pretended to explain the absolute. Acupuncture, which I have already mentioned, is a perfect example of this attitude. No Chinese thinks that it is necessary to 'believe' in systems which have grown up around this ancient empiricism: these are hypotheses which can be discarded if a more elaborate explanation leads to better practice. The only tangible reality is the results obtained. They are more important than all the systems which try to justify them.

This vision of the world is the direct opposite of the logically and rationally constructed system of the West. It is based on an intuition which seeks neither to evade contradictions nor to explain them. Eminently realistic, it aims solely at formulating rules of behaviour which will allow us to be in better harmony with the world and thus to assure our existence in improving it.

TAO: THE WAY AND ESSENTIAL DUALISM

The most ancient books, the canonical books such as the *Nei Ching*, mention *Tao*, the Way, only in passing and in such formulas as 'such is the Way of Heaven'. This moves me to think with Needham that it is necessary to see in its ancient acceptance a kind of 'law of nature' which we cannot know in itself but only in its manifestations. It is necessary to understand law in the sense of a dynamic force of a world essentially in movement. I realise, however, that this term evokes in our ears a dangerously juridical and standardising echo of the Graeco-Romans.

It was only much later, three or four centuries B.C., that the sage Lao Tzu in his book the *Tao Te Ching* (which is at the same time the shortest book and the one most charged with meaning in all Chinese literature), the 'Book of the Way and its Virtue',[6] gives the term an importance which it has borne ever since and a value comparable to the 'word' of St John or λογος in Greek philosophy.

Despite the efforts of the translators to whom I referred in the preface, *Tao Te Ching* is not a manual of philosophy but a mystical and poetic evocation on which we are still meditating.

道可道
非恒道
名可名
非恒名

From the first line the Sage is bent on warning us:
'The Way that can be followed
is not the everlasting Way.
The Name that can be named
is not the everlasting Name.'

Let that be the translation at which we stop. The meaning is clear: to pretend to understand *Tao* is to deny it. We can neither know it nor name it, but only its manifestations. Elusive in its nature, we can only feel its effect: 'Virtue'. The East is almost unanimous in believing that the Absolute is by nature unknowable. Attempts to define it constitute a contradiction and can only excite derision. In the same way that we use electricity without fully understanding its nature, we can only submit to *Tao*'s Virtue which, far from being static, is the dynamic force which rules the Universe. If I were not afraid of philosophical conclusions, I would willingly compare it with Bergson's 'l'elan vital'. The expression 'Life Force' would perhaps be the best equivalent that one can find in English.

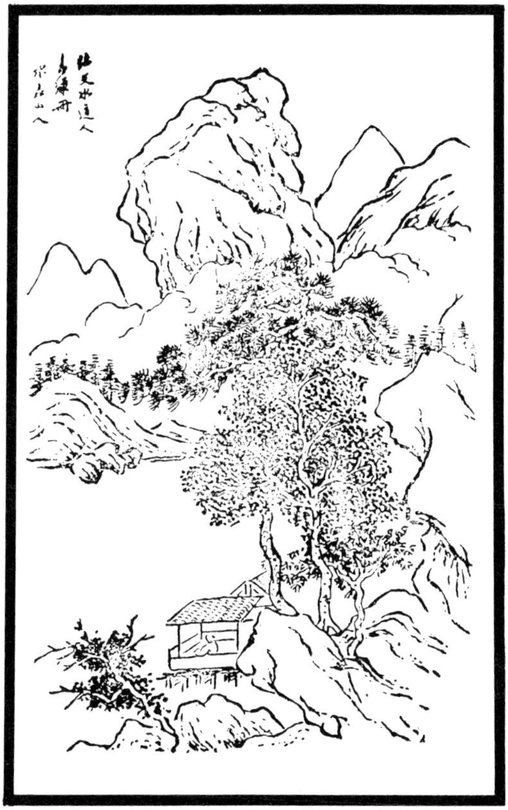

In communion with nature.
The Sage tries to realise within himself the harmony of *Tao*.

Chapter 2

The Interplay of YIN and YANG

The manifestation, the 'Virtue', of *Tao* is illustrated, in a manner both symbolic and charged with meaning, by the famous diagram which expresses essential energy consisting of two opposing yet complementary forces: 太極圖 *T'ai Chi T'u*.[7]

Yin
Feminine
Yielding
Receptive
Even
陰
Yang
Masculine
Dominating
Expanding
Odd
陽

The first character *T'ai* means 'big, extreme, supreme'; the second *Chi* 'the ridge pole of a house, extremity, pole'. It is the term used to designate the North Pole, the axis on which the universe rotates. The third character *T'u* signifies 'design, diagram'. Literally one can translate the whole expression as 'the diagram of the supreme pole', which avoids the inconvenience of the more usual translation as the 'diagram of the Supreme Principle or the Absolute', but which bears philosophical implications not apparent to me.

YIN AND YANG, OR THE ESSENTIAL DUALISM

For the Chinese the existence of this dualism is constantly apparent in the Universe and seems to be inherent in the nature of things: like day and night which seem unflaggingly to generate each other reciprocally. But the originality of the Chinese vision is that, unlike the Manichean view, these two forces are both paradoxical and complementary. Furthermore they are not two distinct principles but two complementary aspects of the same reality: nothing is *Yang* or *Yin* absolutely and one can say that everything possesses a *yin* aspect and a *yang* aspect. As the *Nei Ching* says 'in *yin* there is *yang* and in *yang* there is *yin*', as is clearly shown by the white dot in the *yin* and the black dot in the *yang* in the diagram. It is not concerned with two distinct principles or two elements of a composition, but rather with two vital forces always solidly implicated the one in the other and neither being the simple negation of the other.

The etymology of the two characters is also very instructive.

陰 The character *Yin* signifies the dark 侌 or northern side 阝 of a hill.

陽 The character *Yang* the sunny 昜 or southern side 阝. The inventive spirit of the Chinese has led them to make interminable lists of antithetical principles. Perhaps for reasons of euphony – surely not of courtesy – the feminine *Yin* is named first when the two characters are associated.

For this reason I have used the following list which gives the feminine first and masculine second: equal, unequal; darkness, light; moon, sun; night, day; winter, summer (in North China the little noticed spring and autumn are merely a short transition between the two extremes); cold, heat; north, south; humidity, drought; inertia, activity; rest, work; receptivity, expansion; etc. In popular religions this dualism is expressed by two images: the White Tiger (colour of death and grief) associated with the West and the evening; and the Green Dragon[8] (colour of vegetation) associated with the East and the morning. In the Taoist pantheon there is also the sovereign Mother of the West opposed to the Jade Emperor who resides on the Mountain Peak of the East.

The Taoists emphasise that in the diagram a secant, parallel to the medial axis, will always run through a certain portion of the *Yin* and the *Yang*, but never one or the other in isolation. At the same time, a diameter rotating round the centre will always meet, although unequally distributed, an equivalent proportion of *Yin* and of *Yang*. As with the *Tao* itself, the Sages have never tried to explain *Yin* and *Yang*. They were content to conjure up poetic allegories, like Chuang Tzŭ, who said 'the apogee of *Yin* is passivity; that of *Yang* is fruitful activity. All that exists was produced by the receptivity of the Earth offering itself to Heaven and by the action of Heaven on the Earth.' As the Chinese see it, man is precisely at the meeting point between Heaven and Earth. '*Yin* and *Yang* are products of *Tao*. They influence each other, annihilate each other and reproduce each other reciprocally.'[9]

In a passage of the *Nei Ching* we find: '*Yang* and *Yin* correspond to the Way *(Tao)* of Heaven and Earth . . . Heaven creates itself by means of a concentration of *Yang*, Earth by an accumulation of *Yin*. *Yin* is also calm, *Yang* constantly in motion. *Yang* engenders life, *Yin* maintains it and imposes itself on it. *Yang* kills, *Yin* preserves. *Yang* changes itself in *Yin* in order to create life.'

The movement of these two forces should tend towards equilibrium (but remember, a perfect equilibrium will lead to stagnation and death), even as for a man on a bicycle constant disequilibrium can only be corrected by movement; or, to take an image dear to Mao Tse-tung, the alternate action of a (single) oar makes the boat move and maintains its course by two opposing pressures.

It is worth noting that in the eyes of the masses the Marxist dialectic is seen merely as a new illustration of this dualism which China has known since early antiquity. 矛盾 *mao tun*,[10] the term used to translate the idea of contradiction, combines the lance and the shield, both of which are needed to denote opposition and its complement.

Evil is the imbalance produced by one of the two tendencies becoming predominant to the detriment of the other. Drought is good only in alternation with humidity; otherwise there would be scarcity and famine and, in the opposite case, floods. Neither *Yin* nor *Yang* are good or bad in themselves. Only an excessive predominance of one or the other is dangerous.

This is a vital point in acupunctural diagnosis, to the Chinese all disorders of the body are due to the excessive part played by either *Yin* or *Yang*. To re-establish equilibrium in a sick person, he would be 'toned up' to strengthen a deficiency of energy or, in the opposite case, he would be enfeebled by 'dispersing' any excess of strength.

At the risk of being repetitive, it is important to remember that Chinese thought is the antithesis of Manicheism. For the Chinese, therefore, neither *Yin* nor *Yang* can be evil in itself; they can sin only by excess or by default.

In all destiny the law of life is that *Yin* and *Yang* interpenetrate; but too perfect an equilibrium between them is not desirable, for it would be the equivalent of stagnation.

It is good and normal to find in a man's horoscope a predominance of *Yang*, and of *Yin* in a woman. It is preferable, therefore, for a man to be born in a *Yang* year while, conversely, for a woman a *Yin* year is indicated. But remember, in *Yang* there ought always to be something of *Yin*, and by the same token, *Yin* ought always to contain something of *Yang*. If all the signs defining a man's birthday were *Yang*, it would be almost as dangerous as if they were all *Yin*. The reverse is true for a woman.

This essential dualism is the key to interpretation of every Chinese horoscope. At the same time, it is the most elusive element because it is impossible to reduce it to a rational formula. Some figures of speech or comparisons, as we have seen, can never give us full satisfaction but only some inkling of it.

Neither should we forget that *Yin* and *Yang* must not be regarded solely as aspects of the relationship between masculinity and feminity; we have seen that they have many other aspects. It is very important for the psychological aspect to note that *Yang*, indicative of expansiveness, is a sign of an active *extrovert* nature, while *Yin*, indicating receptivity, almost possessiveness, is the sign of a retiring, contemplative and *introvert* nature.

A very good example of how the Chinese *(honi soit qui mal y pense)* see the relationship between the two principles is the importance which they place on love play and the wisdom which should inform the act of loving.[11]

The Chinese have defined in detail an art of love which, however it may appear to us, is eminently moral, for it aims at complete harmony in sexual union. The Chinese believe that it is the man (expansive *Yang*) who gives himself and risks misusing his *Yang* potential by exhausting it. The woman (receptive *Yin*) on the other hand, is content to receive and to enrich herself by the equilibrium obtained from the *Yang* forces which she has absorbed. In short, the woman tends to exhaust the man through dominating his forces, by her passivity. On the other hand, the stronger and more protracted her enjoyment, the more she liberates the *Yin* elements which the man can then assimilate. Since a young woman is in the fullness of her feminity, it is then that she can most enrich the man who possesses her.

Taoists (who in their search for immortality almost forget the essential moderation of the Chinese) have sometimes tended to accord too great a predominance to the *Yang* forces. Thus they have made a point of using methods to increase as much as possible the pleasure of the woman while delaying to the utmost that of the man. Some even egotistically believe that the ideal is not to produce sperm but to be satisfied with plundering the humours of *Yin*.

In brief the man should apply himself to stimulating the greatest enjoyment in his partner while controlling his own pleasure. This is far from the nonsensical belief that for an oriental the woman is simply a plaything for male lubricity.

Taoists prefer to show the *T'ai Chi T'u* surrounded by eight trigrams which represent all possible combinations of equality and inequality (*Yin* and *Yang*). Joined two by two, these trigrams form the sixty-four sacred hexagrams of the *I Ching*, the 'Book of Changes', which

The Taoist Symbol of the Universe

for the Chinese contains the secret of 'all that is to come'.

In this diagram South, illustrated by the trigram of unbroken lines, is, following the Chinese tradition, placed at the top and represents the extreme *Yang*; and North, illustrated by the trigram of broken lines, at the bottom, and represents the extreme *Yin*.[12]

It is also amusing to note that this book, the '*I Ching*', gave to Leibnitz, who much admired it, the idea of the binary system, from which modern computer science is derived.

Chapter 3

Importance of Divination

For us whose vision of the World is dominated by utility and the desire to possess, it is difficult to understand the psychology of a man for whom the Universe does not consist merely of an inexhaustible reservoir of natural resources. However, for a large part of humanity, Nature constitutes a reality which it is important to respect, for on submission to its law depends our survival and accomplishments.

It is very significant that all artistic interpretation in China – calligraphy and painting, architecture and music – is dominated by the notion of equilibrium and *harmony* and by the search for a profound oneness with Nature.

From what has been said already, it is easy for us to conclude that, for a Chinese, to understand the Universe is not to try to give it an impossibly rational explanation, but to grasp its laws in order that our lives may conform harmoniously with them. To know oneself is to realise the forces which define our personality as well as to play our role in the World on which we depend. To acquire this knowledge constitutes an essentially moral act (and even the only moral act as understood by the Chinese) for it is concerned with realising universal harmony.

In Chinese eyes to sow out of season, for example, is not only useless but dangerous, for it is a disorder. Whatever conforms to order and is done at the right time and under the right conditions is auspicious, expedient and therefore beneficent – all that is disordered is inauspicious, inexpedient and therefore maleficent. *To discover this order is the essential function of divination and a moral activity par excellence.*

It is not by chance that the oldest documents, the oracular inscriptions of the Shang dynasty, dating from about three thousand years ago, record divinatory operations.

To make a comparison which gamblers, such as the Chinese often are, will not challenge, divination helps us to recognise the cards which we hold and therefore helps us to make the most of the odds in our favour. The Chinese, who are fundamentally peasants, have learnt that the success of an action such as sowing (to keep the same example) depends essentially on the period and the way in which it begins. This explains the importance for them of the New Year Holiday whose happy passing is the best guarantee of happiness for the year which is beginning. This is also why the Chinese consider it necessary to consult their horoscopes before undertaking any important action; and it is even recommended that, to be on the safe side, they should follow it up by asking the advice of an expert.

THE VALUE AND LIMITATIONS OF DIVINATION

In the canonical books (the thirteen classics) there are many allusions to methods of divination which prove its importance to the Chinese from the earliest times. But Chinese moderation is clearly shown every time divination is mentioned: it never takes the place of human judgement except when it is resorted to in doubtful cases. Thus in the chapter of the *Shu Ching* entitled 'the Great Plan', it is said:

'If you have any doubts about any great matter, consult with your own heart [this refers to the Emperor]; consult with your nobles and officers; consult with the masses of the people; consult the tortoise and milfoil . . .[13] if there is unanimity, the enterprise will succeed . . . If you, the tortoise and the milfoil all agree, while the nobles and common people oppose, the result will be fortunate. If the nobles and officers, the tortoise and the milfoil all agree, while you oppose and the common people oppose, the result will be fortunate. If the common people, the tortoise and the milfoil all agree, while you and the nobles oppose, the result will be fortunate. If you and the tortoise agree, while the milfoil, the nobles and officers, and the common people oppose, internal operations will be fortunate and external operations will be unlucky. When the tortoise and the milfoil are both opposed to the views of men, there will be good fortune in stillness, and active operations will be unlucky.'[14]

The use of divination does not dispense with reflection for divination cannot give absolutely certain replies. Nevertheless its indications should be treated with respect. In the same book, in the chapter entitled 'The counsels of the great *Yü*', the Emperor refuses to return to the oracles: '. . . my mind was determined in the first place. I consulted and deliberated with all my ministers and people, and they were of one accord with me. The spirits signified their assent, the tortoise and grass have both concurred. Divination, when fortunate, may not be repeated.' Clearly it is quite different when the oracles are unfavourable.[15]

THE THREE GREAT OCCASIONS

For a Chinese it is imperative to study carefully the eight signs of his destiny on the three great occasions of existence:

BIRTH, MARRIAGE, DEATH

Birth

It is necessary to know if the arrival in the World of a newly-born child will be auspicious for its family. If not, adoption (sometimes merely fictitious) by another family, for whom the child would be auspicious, is resorted to. The idea is to change destiny by thus modifying the identity of the child. In extreme cases the original identity must remain secret: thus, for example, no one has ever revealed to me the true identity of my wife.

Marriage

On all evidence, the union of two destinies and above all, in Chinese eyes, the introduction of a foreign element into the bosom of the family must be surrounded by the greatest precautions. The first duty of a marriage broker (necessary for all marriages for, in an adverse case, not to go through with the project would cost serious loss of face to one party or the other) is therefore to make a minutely detailed comparison of the eight signs of each of the future partners. In common parlance, to entertain a marriage project is called 'to exchange the eight signs'. The comparison is moreover treated with the greatest discretion, for knowledge of this secret key to character by a third party can be dangerous.

Death

That death does not cut family links between the deceased and the living is of prime importance in China. It is essential that the conditions for the last voyage should be established in the most favourable manner both for the departed and for his family. Minute precautions are taken to ensure that any influence the slightest bit inauspicious should be avoided by carefully comparing the eight signs of the deceased with the signs of the day and the hour of the obsequies, and by choosing the appropriate position and orientation of the grave. Those whose presence would be unfavourable are banned from the cortege: thus a good friend of mine once asked me with some embarrassment not to attend his father's funeral because I was born in the Year of the Rat, and my presence would have been undesirable on the day and at the hour appointed.

On any occasion which they consider sufficiently important, the Chinese turn to a 'specialist' to whom naturally they have to communicate their date of birth, much as we in the West might show our X-ray photograph to a physician. In the ordinary course of events, however, the calendar suffices for the recognition of favourable or unfavourable indications, since each day is given a list of recommended actions or the opposite: to determine a suitable time for a betrothal, a marriage, a funeral, or whether to go fishing, lay the foundation of a house, have one's hair cut, take a bath, set out on a journey and so on. Auspicious or inauspicious hours are also shown. A British businessman whom I knew in the Far East told me that he always consulted an almanac before arranging a meeting with a Chinese. Experience had taught him that there was not even a one per cent chance of the other person turning up if the hour had been declared inauspicious.

Chapter 4

Time and the Calendar

THE EMPEROR AND THE CALENDAR

The establishment of the calendar was the most important of the Emperor's duties, the one which in every way justified his role and his prerogatives and for which he was invested with the Mandate of Heaven. To improve the accuracy of the calendar he did not hesitate to ask advice even from foreign barbarians – at first Muslims and later, in the middle of the seventeenth century, Jesuits. As intermediary between Heaven and Earth, the Emperor had above all to establish a relationship or to make contact as we might say today. On the 'Altar of Heaven' during the day of the Winter Solstice it was his duty to render the thanks of his people to Heaven; as it was also in the 'Temple of Heaven' at the beginning of Spring, to pray to Heaven and make his 'requests for the year to come'.

The observance of the rites in the most scrupulous manner had the magical power of ensuring order in the World, *T'ien Hsia* 'that which is under Heaven' as the Chinese commonly call the Universe. It is true that this very strict compulsion has relaxed over the centuries, but the principle retains its force.

The Monthly Residences of the Son of Heaven

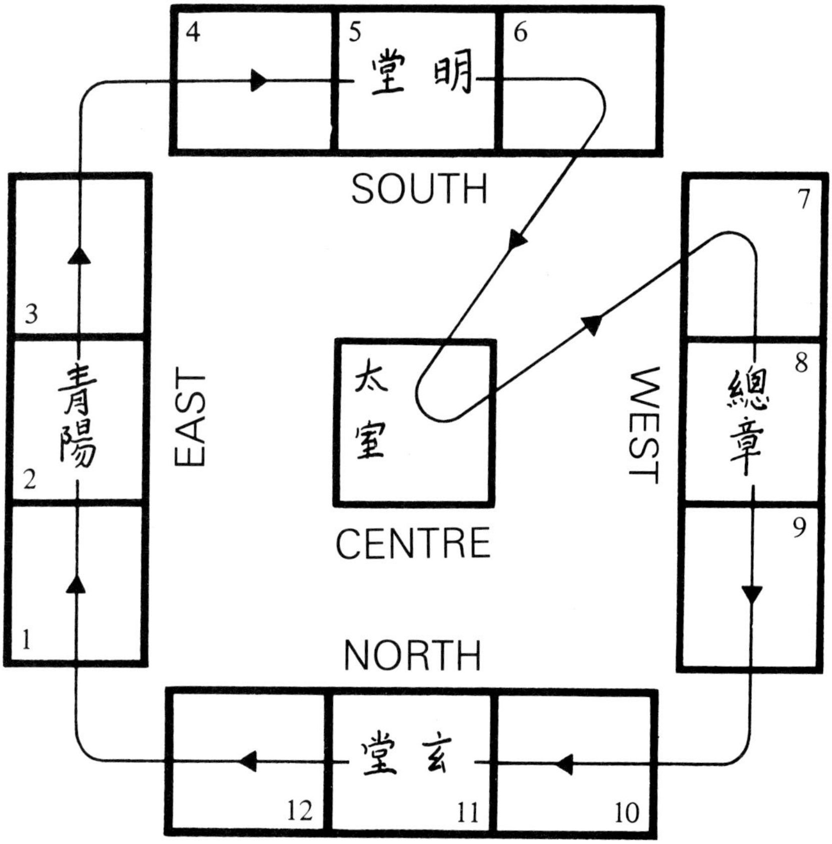

4
5
6
明堂
SOUTH
7
3
青陽
EAST
太室
WEST
總章
8
2
CENTRE
9
1
NORTH
玄堂
12
11
10

In his choice of a monthly residence, the Emperor follows the progress of the Sun. In conformity with Chinese usage, we have put South at the top of the diagram.

Following the *Yüeh Ling*, the Emperor had, symbolically and in accordance with the Seasons, to live successively in different parts of his palace. In Spring he lived for a month at a time in each of three parts of the *Ch'ing Yang*, 'Green *Yang*', Palace situated in the East part of the imperial residence. In conformity with the Agent Wood he had to dress in green, eat corn and mutton, etc. . . . In Summer he lived similarly in the southern parts of the residence, *Ming T'ang*, 'Palace of Clarity', dressed in red and ate peas and chickens. The Agent Earth then intervened. The texts do not indicate clearly the period for this, but tradition says the dog days. He had to live in the central part of his residence, the *T'ai Shih*, 'the Supreme Hall', which was also the Temple of Ancestors, dress in yellow and eat millet and beef. It is characteristic that, when these rites became obsolete, yellow (the colour of Earth) became the imperial colour thus confirming the primordial importance of the Agent Earth, the Centre, which produces all the others.[16] The *Nei Ching*, on the other hand, indicates clearly that the Agent Earth is dominant in the third month of each season.

In Autumn the Emperor lived successively in the three parts of the Palace of the West, *Tsung Chang*, 'Hall of assembled Beauty', where he had to wear white clothes and eat sesame and dog. Finally, during the Winter months he lived in the Palace of the North, *Hsüan T'ang*, 'the Palace of Darkness' or of Mystery, wore black and ate sorghum and pork.

The *Yüeh Ling* enumerates a long list of disasters which would not fail to occur if the Emperor dared to interpret the rites at the wrong time.

Some authors think that the Emperor had, in the order of the seasons, to make a ritual visit to the eastern, southern, western and northern parts of his Empire, while returning to the centre after each visit. Others believe that he had to make a pilgrimage to each of the Holy Mountain Peaks of the four points (of the compass) without forgetting the fifth in the Centre.

It was for him to open the ploughing season by tracing the first furrow on the day and at the hour appointed, and to announce the opening of the fishing and hunting seasons.

THE SOLAR CALENDAR

In China two calendars are used for astrological purposes, a solar calendar and a lunar one. We shall discuss the lunar calendar later on in this chapter. The solar calendar is the only one used in connection with the cosmic order and is the one preferred by Chinese astrologers and acupuncturists.

The commentaries of the *Nei Ching* indicate a year computing 365 days and 25 *k'o* (quarters of an hour), i.e. 365 ¼ days, thereby exceeding the real year by 14 minutes and 12 seconds.[17]

Chinese astrologers also use what they called the 'Great Year', *T'ai Sui*, based on the cycle of Jupiter which takes approximately twelve years to revolve around the Sun. *T'ai Sui* describes both the planet and its revolution; and, as we shall see, the duodenary cycle is based on this privileged period of twelve years, which allows the establishment of a relationship with the Western signs of the Zodiac whenever Jupiter resides in them. Although the Chinese have not expressly made comparisons between the *T'ai Sui* and the signs of the Zodiac, it may be of interest to Western astrologers if we do so here. It is true that such a comparison cannot be exact astronomically speaking, but the same could be said about the commentaries of Western astrologers when they use the Zodiac whose signs change every two thousand years or so.[18]

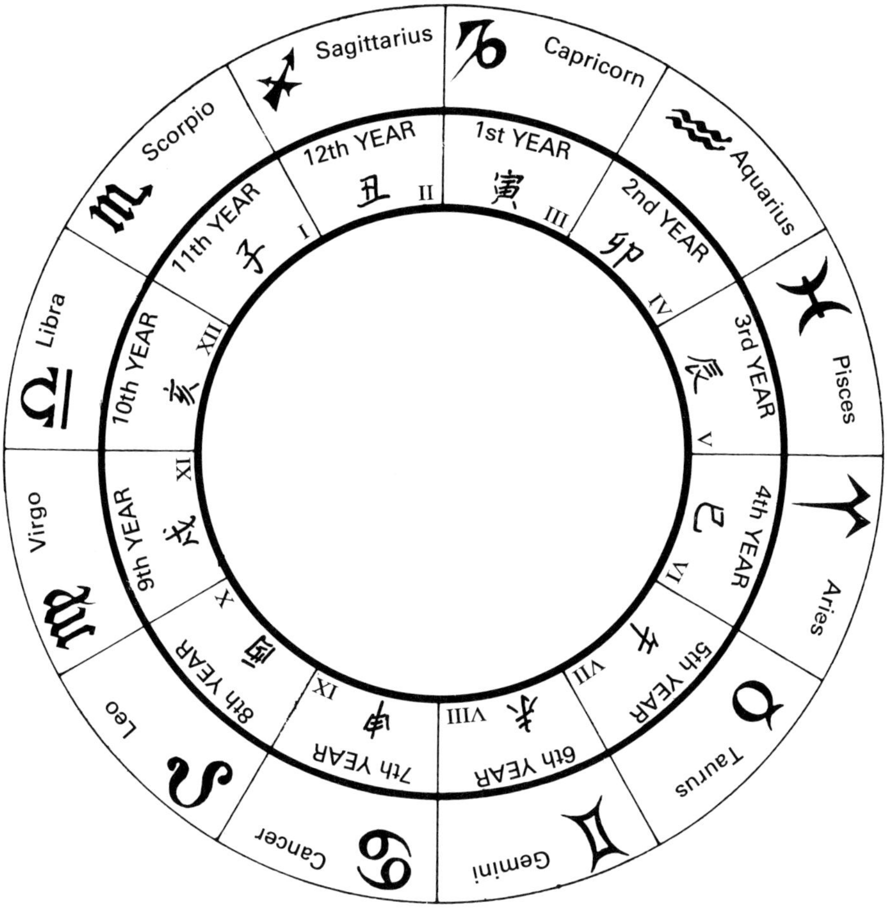
Sagittarius
Capricorn
Aquarius
Pisces
Aries
Taurus
Gemini
Cancer
Leo
Virgo
Libra
Scorpio
1st YEAR
寅
III
2nd YEAR
卯
IV
3rd YEAR
辰
V
4th YEAR
巳
VI
5th YEAR
午
VII
6th YEAR
未
VIII
7th YEAR
申
IX
8th YEAR
酉
X
9th YEAR
戌
XI
10th YEAR
亥
XII
11th YEAR
子
I
12th YEAR
丑
II

The Cycle of Jupiter

The year is finally divided into twenty-four 'solar terms',[19] each lasting about fifteen days. They begin at the Winter solstice and, grouped two by two, cover the same period as the Zodiac. Very important for defining the Seasons, they are also the basis for the calculation of the twelve solar months (periods) of the year in traditional Chinese astronomy. Properly speaking the astrological year begins therefore with the Winter solstice, the establishment of which is the fundamental point of departure for all astronomical calculations.

Nevertheless, as we have seen, Chinese astrologers prefer to base their calculations for the horoscopes of individuals on the date of the establishment of Spring (4/5 February) – see page 61 – i.e. the fourth term of the following table (p. 20). Each succeeding solar month also starts with an even numbered term: the second period with the sixth term, the third with the eighth . . . and so on till the twelfth which begins with the second term.

The names given to these twenty-four solar terms are ancient. For any one who has lived in China, they illustrate very well the sharp powers of observation possessed by the Chinese people. Eight of these terms are considered the most important beginning with the fourth, tenth, sixteenth and twenty-second, which for the Chinese indicate respectively the beginning of the four seasons; then the first, seventh, thirteenth and nineteenth which indicate the solstices and equinoxes.

THE TWENTY-FOUR SOLAR TERMS

	Days		Common Names of Positions	Entry of the Sun in:
1	22 Dec	冬至	*Winter Solstice*	1° Capricorn
2	5 Jan	小寒	*Little Cold*	16° Capricorn
3	20 Jan	大寒	*Great Cold*	1° Aquarius
4	4 Feb	立春	*Beginning of Spring*	16° Aquarius
5	19 Feb	雨水	*Rain Water*	1° Pisces
6	5 Mar	驚蟄	*Movement of Insects*	16° Pisces
7	20 Mar	春分	*Spring Equinox*	1° Aries
8	5 Apr	清明	*Serene Clarity*	16° Aries
9	20 Apr	穀雨	*Grain Rains*	1° Taurus
10	5 May	立夏	*Beginning of Summer*	16° Taurus
11	21 May	小滿	*Little Surfeit*	1° Gemini
12	6 Jun	芒種	*Grain in Ear*	16° Gemini
13	21 Jun	夏至	*Summer Solstice*	1° Cancer
14	7 Jul	小暑	*Little Heat*	16° Cancer
15	23 Jul	大暑	*Great Heat*	1° Leo
16	7 Aug	立秋	*Beginning of Autumn*	16° Leo
17	23 Aug	處暑	*Heat Ceasing*	1° Virgo
18	7 Sep	白露	*White Dew*	16° Virgo
19	23 Sep	秋分	*Autumn Equinox*	1° Libra
20	8 Oct	寒露	*Cold Dew*	16° Libra
21	23 Oct	霜降	*Frost Descends*	1° Scorpio
22	7 Nov	立冬	*Beginning of Winter*	16° Scorpio
23	22 Nov	小雪	*Little Snow*	1° Sagittarius
24	7 Dec	大雪	*Great Snow*	16° Sagittarius

This table was inspired by Havret. It is accurate to plus or minus one day.

THE LUNAR-SOLAR CALENDAR, OR THE PEASANT ALMANAC

It is quite evident that the solar calendar, which is satisfactory enough for astronomical needs and for the establishment of abstract dating, is far too brief for an agricultural population whose chief need is to find in the almanac practical indications which are immediately usable. Besides it would be unthinkable that peasants, who are such attentive observers of nature, should not pay attention to lunations and the phases of the moon; it is then a lunar calendar which the Chinese use as a basis for calculating time. The solar calendar of astrologers has never supplanted it, and even now all attempts by the Chinese Government to eliminate it have been frustrated. In fact the calendar in present use, the one which was promulgated by the Emperor, is a lunar-solar calendar comprising a convenient conjugation of the two systems. The twenty-four solar terms are, moreover, very useful for agriculture.

The problem of reconciling lunar months with the solar year is certainly not easy, but the Chinese have solved it with elegance. The synodic lunar month, that is to say the time elapsing between two consecutive new moons, lasts 29 days, 12 hours, and 44 minutes. This is a mean figure, since the influence of the Sun, of Jupiter and of Venus can modify the duration by nearly one hour. 12 moons (I use that term rather than months to avoid confusion) make therefore 354 days, 8 hours, 48 minutes, or 10 days, 21 hours shorter than the solar year.

As a moon must consist of an exact number of days, there will be 'great moons' of 30 days, and 'little moons' of 29 days. The 'common years' will therefore have 354 days (with 6 great moons) or 355 days (with 7 great moons).

In order to re-establish the equilibrium with the solar year, it is necessary from time to time to add an intercalary moon or 'embolism', and it has been calculated that there should be 7 'embolisms' in a period of 19 years. This is the cycle known to the Greeks and the Hebrews as the cycle of Meton. In China the embolismic years are the 3rd, 6th, 9th, 11th, 14th, 17th and the 19th of the cycle. The cycles of 19 years for the end of the 19th century and for the 20th century begin in 1890, 1909, 1928, 1947, 1966, 1985, 2004, etc.

Accordingly embolismic years have 383 (6 great moons), 384 (7 great moons) or 385 days (8 great moons). The method of intercalating an embolismic moon has changed greatly through the ages. I shall content myself with showing the method now in force as follows:

It is imperative that the Spring equinox should fall in the second moon, the Summer solstice in the fifth, the Autumn equinox in the eighth and the Winter solstice in the eleventh moon. It is then necessary, whatever the length of the year, that the 1st, 2nd and 3rd moons should roughly correspond with Spring, the 4th, 5th and 6th moons with Summer, the 7th, 8th and 9th moons with Autumn, the 10th, 11th and 12th moons with Winter. Intercalary moons do not contain days on which signs of the Zodiac change. An embolismic moon has no personality of its own; it keeps the number of the moon which immediately precedes it. If, for example, it is placed after the 4th moon it will be called the '4th embolismic moon' and will be affected by the same cyclic signs.

The 1st, 11th and 12th moons are never duplicated for they correspond with the shortest winter stations. Whenever an embolismic moon ought normally to be placed after the 12th moon, it is postponed to after the second moon of the following year. This happened notably in 1889, 1908, 1927, 1946 and 1965. In practice the moon is duplicated when its number in the order corresponds with the number of days remaining between the Winter solstice and the sygyzy which follows. If the number exceeds twelve, the remainder only is used.

The Chinese New Year's Day is not fixed therefore, but may be on any date between

21 January and 20 February. Thus, when we compare a Chinese year with the Western year, it must be remembered that the days between 1 January and Chinese New Year's Day belong to the preceding year.

In China there are numerous ways of grouping years in longer or shorter periods. We have already seen the 'Great Year', the cycle of twelve years which corresponds with one revolution of Jupiter round the sun and also the period of nineteen years which is the basis of the cycle of embolismic months. There is another period of thirty years called *Shih* 世, wrongly translated by 'century'. The most interesting period is one of sixty years, which corresponds with the sexagenary cycle and is called *Yüan* 元 (see p. 23).

THE TWELVE HOURS

All Chinese agree on attaching the greatest importance to the precise hour of your birth when the fairies bend over your cradle, to mix Eastern folklore with Western! A horoscope is incomplete if it does not contain this element which in a way puts the final touch to your personality. It is also essential at this time that the augurs should judge if the newly born will be welcome in the family where it sees the light of day.

The hours of the day number twelve and in their connection the cycle of the Twelve Terrestrial Branches is the most significant.

Some experts associate this cycle with the twelve animals thus completing the portrait indicated by the animal of the year and permitting a more elaborate study of each person's character.

A Chinese hour contains two of our hours and is divided into two parts, each of which is equal to a Western hour. The first is called the 'beginning hour', the second the 'exact hour'. The day begins at midnight, but the first Chinese hour *Tzŭ* 子 begins at 23.00 and therefore straddles two days, as do the signs belonging to it.

In early times the day was divided into ten periods, *shih* 時, which themselves divided into ten *k'o* 刻. It was only during the Han 漢 Dynasty, probably in the second century AD, that the twelve hours were adopted. But the division into one hundred fractions remained, the 1st and the 7th hour each counting ten divisions. It was in the K'ang Hsi era in 1670 that Father Verbiest, the Jesuit advisor to the Emperor, persuaded him to change the value of the *k'o* into 1/96th of a day thus making it equivalent to the Western quarter hour. Later the quarter hour was divided into fifteen minutes, exactly identical to the Western one.

We have therefore the following table of hours:

1 子 *tzŭ*	beginning	23h		7 午 *wu*	beginning	11h
	exact	0h			exact	12h
2 丑 *ch'ou*	beginning	1h		8 未 *wei*	beginning	13h
	exact	2h			exact	14h
3 寅 *yin*	beginning	3h		9 申 *shen*	beginning	15h
	exact	4h			exact	16h
4 卯 *mao*	beginning	5h		10 酉 *yu*	beginning	17h
	exact	6h			exact	18h
5 辰 *ch'en*	beginning	7h		11 戌 *hsü*	beginning	19h
	exact	8h			exact	20h
6 巳 *ssŭ*	beginning	9h		12 亥 *hai*	beginning	21h
	exact	10h			exact	22h

Chapter 5

The Sexagenary Cycle and its Components

THE SEXAGENARY CYCLE OF THE SIXTY COMBINATIONS

In current parlance a date is announced in the simplest way by indicating the year, the month, the day and the hour, for the Chinese always go from the general to the particular. In imperial times the year was identified by a number within an Era which constituted a reign: the 3rd Year of *K'ang Hsi*, the 5th Year of *Ch'ien Lung*, etc.

In 1911 the Imperial Era was replaced by the word Republic, a usage which T'aiwan has kept, 1977 for example being for them the 66th Year of the Republic. In their desire to abolish ancient customs, the Communists did not wish to create a new era (at least in the calendar) and they adopted instead the Western calendar. But till now they have not been able to eradicate the old system; and thus, after several attempts to suppress the traditional dates in the newspapers (as happened at the beginning of 1977) they have returned once more to the solution of citing concurrently both calendars, the 'common' calendar and the 'peasant' calendar.

However, time, disregarding events and political changes, moves inexorably on its course. Nothing can alter it; and each moment through the years, months, days and hours is marked in regular succession by the eight signs which identify it and, in a way, attribute to it an individuality by giving it a name.

This name is the combination of the four names of the four binomials. The name of each binomial comprises two characters: one of the denary cycle and one of the duodenary cycle, which together form the sexagenary cycle.

In this book we have found it convenient to use the term binomial. However the Chinese, who are so aware of the vital importance of the binomials, call them 四柱, *Ssŭ Chu*, the 'Four Pillars' of destiny.[20]

The sexagenary cycle, which is reported to have been created by the semi-legendary Emperor Huang Ti, the 'Yellow Emperor' and wise organiser of the Empire, goes back unchanged to 2677 BC. Its basic element is an era of sixty years (following the sexagenary cycle) grouped in threes, thus making a longer era of one hundred and eighty years. The three cycles of this period are called the three *Yüan*, that is to say the three 'beginnings' which are known respectively as the 'higher beginning', the 'middle beginning' and the 'lower beginning': 上元 *Shang Yüan* 中元 *Chung Yüan* 下元 *Hsia Yüan*.

We are now (1982) in the final *Yüan* of the 26th era. The opening *Yüan* of the 27th era begins on 4 February 1984.

One may note that even numbered Western years correspond with odd numbered Chinese years (*Yang*): 1924 = year 1 of the cycle; and odd numbered Western years to even numbered Chinese years (*Yin*): 1983 = year 60 of the cycle.

The eight signs of our destiny belong to two series of characters which we shall study in greater detail: the ten 'Celestial Stems' and the twelve 'Terrestrial Branches'. The denary series, which is the oldest, sees its signs repeat themselves six times in a cycle while those of the duodenary cycle repeat themselves five times. All the characters of odd numbers in one series *(Yang)* are necessarily associated in the course of a cycle with all the odd numbers of the other series. The same goes for the characters of even number *(Yin)*.

THE VALUE OF THE SIGN

To understand the importance to the Chinese of the eight signs, it is necessary to digress briefly to explain what they mean to them. For Westerners, preoccupied with reason and logic, have nearly lost sight of what for the Chinese is obvious: every written sign and every gesture has its own value. Man has always believed in the power of magical gestures. A shaman tries to impose his ascendancy on others by apeing a person, a thing or an action in a performance indissolubly uniting music, dance and song; or, to take another example, an incantation inscribed on a stone confers on it a supreme efficacy. There is little doubt now that this is the meaning which must be given to the rock drawings of les Eyzies or the Altamira caves.

To give a name to, or to describe by gesture or drawing, is magically to possess a thing. In the Bible, God names the stars and empowers Adam to name the beings of Creation. The supreme moment in the Old Testament is when God reveals to Moses both his nature and his name, the name for which the Hebrews had so much reverence that they hid its true pronunciation. This was not only out of respect but because the magical use of this name was the supreme offence: the essential 'sacrilege'. Christians have forgotten that this was the true meaning of God's Commandment, inscribed on the tablets of the Law, which forbade the taking of God's name in vain.

In the same way, Chinese respect for the personal name is associated with the fear of seeing it used magically. The use of the personal name is reserved to intimates only, but in other relationships a Chinese can choose or be given many different names. This multiplicity of names for one individual is often confusing and makes the reading of a popular novel rather difficult for a Westerner. After the death of an important personage, he will solemnly be given a posthumous name: thus Sun Yatsen since his death has been called Sun Chungshan. The name of the Emperor was never known by the people and the literate were forbidden by a taboo to use the characters of the August Name. Thus the ideogram *hsüan* 玄 'mysterious', much used in Taoist literature, was forbidden from the time of the Ch'ien Lung era to the Republic (1911). It had either to be mutilated as 玄, or replaced by another character 元 *(Yüan)*, vaguely equivalent to it. The confusions which arise from this are obvious.

By the way, the terms Ch'ien Lung or K'ang Hsi are not the personal names of Emperors as is often believed; they are auspicious expressions chosen after consultation with sages to designate their reigns. In one unfortunate period it even happened that an Emperor changed the reign-name which seemed to him from experience to have been ill chosen. No doubt he did not forget to chastise his ignorant adviser.[21]

The greatest mark of love which a resident of a 'tea house' can give you is not to grant you her favours (which would be done parsimoniously anyway) but to reveal her personal name to you, thereby becoming your intimate and putting herself at your mercy.

In China there is enormous respect for the written word. The imperial seal was venerated as if it was the person of the Sovereign, and even a visiting card is received with two hands with the greatest respect. Unless it is done for a deliberate purpose, written documents are not burnt for fear of conferring on them a redoubtable and unforeseeable magical power. In South China there used to be charitable societies which took it upon themselves to bury old printed matter decently. And it is told that an old missionary was nearly lynched when, in the most disrespectful way of all, he was found to be using bits of newspaper as lavatory paper. His life was saved when his old assistant agreed to make atonement for the 'sin' by swallowing a bowl of the substance which had been the cause of the impious crime.

It is worth emphasising the fact that the oldest known Chinese ideograms, going back nearly four thousand years, are 'oracular inscriptions'. They consist of bits of tortoise shell or of ox shoulder blades, now fossilised, found at Anyang. On them the royal soothsayers of the Shang dynasty wrote their predictions and, in order to assess the accuracy of their art, the results obtained.[22]

Blinded by the increasing importance placed by Western civilisation on everything which brings us happiness and wealth, nowadays we see the World around us as no more than an object to be dominated by our intelligence. In this context words, themselves derived from algebraic signs, are no longer simply a tool for understanding the Universe, but an instrument by which we can make it our own. I believe that it will be of infinite benefit to us if we rediscover the true value of the 'sign' and thus become truly aware of man's place in the Universe. For a poet each word has its own life and evocative force even as for a painter each stroke of the brush is full of creative power.

For those who look at life in this way possession is mixed with respect. It is therefore only apparently paradoxical to affirm that our prehistoric ancestors probably felt a fearful touch of respect and almost veneration for the animals which they hunted and on whom their survival depended. It would not perhaps be a bad thing if we, rationalists as we are, were to feel a certain humility towards the Universe which gives us life.

THE CYCLIC CHARACTERS

The two series of characters which form the sexagenary cycle are somewhat poetically called 'the ten Celestial Stems' 天干 *T'ien Kan* and 'the twelve Terrestrial Branches' 地支 *Ti Chih*. But the tradition is clear, and the *Nei Ching* is quite precise that 6 is the number of Heaven and 5 the number of Earth: thus the Celestial Stems (5 × 2) condition the Earth and the Terrestrial Branches (6 × 2) Heaven. Granet considers that this 'significant inversion attests to the interdependence of the two series'. Clearly one may think of Heaven ruling Earth and of Earth in return influencing Heaven. While not entirely satisfactory, this explanation conforms to the idea of the interdependence of *Yin* and *Yang*. I am, however, somewhat sceptical when an attempt is made to give a philosophical interpretation to a fact of this kind.

Granted the importance accorded to the cyclic characters, it would be logical to suppose that these characters, which were certainly not chosen by chance, were charged with meaning and symbolism. Unhappily their origin has been lost in the darkness of the past and it has to be acknowledged that, with the exception of two or three of them, no satisfactory etymology can be given. It is indeed surprising to the Western mind that the tradition of such important and fundamental ideas should have been forgotten. However, I suspect that this has happened because these characters were never thought of in isolation but always in their relationships with each other. It does not occur to most Chinese to try to penetrate the symbolism of these familiar ideograms any more than most Westerners would try to pierce the mystery of the shape of an algebraic symbol. They are preoccupied with the practical utility of things rather than wasting time in studying their nature.

In spite of detailed research and the collation of many dictionaries and the works of linguists, astrologers and sinologues, the results which I have obtained are meagre and deceptive. However, I give them below for what they are worth.

The Ten Celestial Stems

The signs which constitute the Ten Celestial Stems are amongst the oldest Chinese characters known. In fact they figure in the oracular inscriptions, where they are linked to the calendar (they indicate the ten days of the period which was equivalent to the week). In a very simple way they are associated two by two (alternatively *yang* and *yin*) with an Agent which has made some people think, notably Saussure, that they are no more than a simple development of the 'theory of the Five Elements'. This seems improbable for they appear in texts much earlier than the Five Agents.[23]

Some authors have found that the etymology of these ten characters show, with some evidence, a link with the annual period to which they belong. For my part I would be more cautious.

Interpretation of the Ten Celestial Stems

From the beginning the Ten Celestial Stems were linked to days as has been amply demonstrated by the study of oracular inscriptions, the oldest known Chinese texts. Today the stems, which are associated in pairs with the Five Agents and are alternately *yang* (odd) and *yin* (even), are in principle linked with the seasons; but they rarely coincide with them or with the duodenary cycle of months and hours.

associated with Wood (and therefore with the beginning, with Spring)

1) 甲 *chia* *yang* — (ancient form 甲) whose shape represents a bud in its protective husk, at the point where it is breaking out.

2) 乙 *yi* *yin* — (ancient form 乚) representation of a sprout leaving the bud, a symbol of blossoming.

According to the *Yüeh Ling*, it is naturally auspicious to be born in Spring on a day whose signs embrace one of these characters.

associated with Fire (and therefore with ripening, with Summer)

3) 丙 *ping* *yang* — (ancient form 丙) fire in the house, concentration and domestication of the power of fire.

4) 丁 *ting* *yin* ㇆ — (ancient form 个) the sting of the bee. According to one commentary, in Summer its sting burns like fire – or rather a nail, the result of the action of fire with the help of which the nail is made. Note that this character today has the meaning of robustness and solidity.

The Summer days marked by these characters are especially auspicious.

associated with Earth (and therefore with full ripening, with the Dog Days)

5) 戊 *wu* *yang* — (ancient form 戊) representation of a hand 又 holding a cutting instrument 戈 in the action of cutting something) : the idea of reaping. Some com-

mentators believe that this character has replaced another signifying flourishing, blooming.

6) 己 *chi* (ancient form 己) this character originally represented the thread of woof
yin and warp. According to the gloss it would signify full bloom.

The presence of one of these characters in the signs of the day is especially auspicious during the dog days.

associated with Metal (and therefore with ageing, with Autumn)

7) 庚 *keng* (ancient form 庚) a clear representation of two hands, one on the left, one
yang on the right, holding or waving something. Wieger says it is the action of pounding rice. Another commentator says harvesting and garnering.

8) 辛 *hsin* (ancient form 辛) idea of offence and punishment – the Autumn, it is
yin suggested, is the time of capital executions. It now signifies bitterness and thus 'the sadness which grips the soul at the approach of Winter'.

If the signs of a day in Autumn contain one of these characters it will be very auspicious.

associated with Water (and therefore with old age, with death, with Winter)

9) 壬 *jen* (ancient form 壬) picture of a man carrying a load in the Chinese manner
yang on the two ends of a pole. Fatigue of a man who carries a load, it is said; one commentator sees it as a symbol of fecundity.

10) 癸 *kuei* (ancient form 癸) matting or decorations made of grass on which were
yin placed sacrifices offered to ancestors as an act of thanksgiving.

In winter the most auspicious days are those on which one of these characters appears in the signs of the days.

These interpretations are traditional and as such deserve to be noted. It must be emphasised that the value attributed to them still lies in their relationship with the day. Shorter horoscopes often take account only of the 'Celestial Stem' character of the day and the two signs of the hour. This is also the case when choosing the most favourable time for acupunctural treatment.

In their relationship with each other and with the Terrestrial Branches, the Celestial Stems have the same affinities and repulsions as the Agents to which they are linked. There is, however, an exception for it is admitted, as indicated in the chart (see page 78), that the opposing signs on the circle have a particular *harmony* in their affinities.

Although 甲 *Chia* (Wood, *yang*) dominates, it is in harmony with 己 *Chi* (Earth, *yin*)

Although 丙 *Ping* (Fire, *yang*) dominates, it is in harmony with 辛 *Hsin* (Metal, *yin*)

Although 戊 *Wu* (Earth, *yang*) dominates, it is in harmony with 癸 *Kuei* (Water, *yin*)

Although 庚 *Keng* (Metal, *yang*) dominates, it is in harmony with 乙 *Yi* (Wood, *yin*)

Although 壬 *Jen* (Water, *yang*) dominates, it is in harmony with 丁 *Ting* (Fire, *yin*)

This seems to be in perfect conformity with the relationship of the two sexes.

The Twelve Terrestrial Branches

These are, we know, associated with Heaven(!). Much less ancient than the ten stems, it seems that they did not appear in the texts until about the fifth century BC. They were first used to designate the twelve hours of the day (the Chinese hour is in fact equivalent to two of ours) then the twelve months and each of the twelve years of the Jupiter cycle.

Their relationships with the Five Agents, moreover, were not so easy to establish as those of the ten stems since the agreement between 5 and 10 is easier to establish than that between 5 and 12. It is not surprising, therefore, that several systems have been suggested. Some, notably amongst the acupuncturists, were content to associate the twelve branches in groups of three with the Seasons and points of the compass, and thus with Wood, Fire, Metal and Water. There remained the Centre as the Agent Earth, omnipresent and timeless.

But the astrologers as a body arrived at a different solution: Wood, Fire, Metal and Water each received a share of two successive branches; the four remaining branches, intercalated one by one between each group were allotted to Earth. This arrangement gives the following alliances:

III 寅 *Yin* (odd, therefore *yang*) and IV 卯 *Mao (yin)* are associated with Wood, Spring and the East.

V 辰 *Ch'en (yang)* with Earth and marks the return to the Centre.

VI 巳 *Ssŭ (yin)* and VII 午 *Wu (yang)* with Fire, the Summer and the South.

VIII 未 *Wei (yin)* with Earth and returns to the Centre.

IX 申 *Shen (yang)* and X 酉 *Yu (yin)* with Metal, Autumn and the West.

XI 戌 *Hsü (yang)* with Earth and returns to the Centre.

XII 亥 *Hai (yin)* and I 子 *Tzŭ (yang)* with Water, Winter and the North.

II 丑 *Ch'ou (yin)* with Earth and returns to the Centre.

It will be noticed that the Agents of a season do not necessarily follow in *yang* and *yin* order, but a return to the Centre after each Season is perfectly logical. It could explain the period when the Emperor returned to the Centre of his palace and wore yellow.

Yin marks the beginning of the series and not *Tzŭ* for the latter belongs to the winter solstice (the beginning of the astronomical year). The series of the Jupiter cycle also begins with *Yin*.

Interpretation of the Twelve Terrestrial Branches

Although they appear later, the etymology of the twelve branches is perhaps even more imprecise than that of the stems, and the subject seems to have quite escaped the attention of commentators. It is true that in practice their place is often taken by the twelve animals which have the advantage of appealing far more to popular imagination. They are, however, the principal elements for the study of the year, the months and the hours.

I 子 *tzŭ* (ancient form ) picture of a small child; birth, seed, germ, beginning.
yang

II *yin*	丑	*ch'ou*	(ancient form ) bound hand, idea of binding, it is suggested, to help growth at the beginning and to sustain the young plant.
III *yang*	寅	*yin*	(ancient form ) under a roof, two hands joined in greeting, whence reverence, respect; visits and greetings joined in celebration of Spring and the New Year.
IV *yin*	卯	*mao*	(ancient form 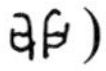) an open door: reception of Spring.
V *yang*	辰	*ch'en*	(ancient form ) picture of a woman whose hands hide her belly: pregnant and timid.
VI *yin*	巳	*ssŭ*	(ancient form ) fully formed embryo. If this meaning is equated with that of the twelfth sign, it is the seventh month of gestation.
VII *yang*	午	*wu*	(ancient form ) opposition, struggle, the moment when *yang* reaches its highest point and arouses the opposition of *yin*.
VIII *yin*	未	*wei*	(ancient form ) a big tree with fully grown branches.
IX *yang*	申	*shen*	(ancient form ) two hands holding a rope, expansion; another way of writing this word suggests the struggle of the two alternate principles (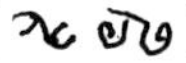) which engender the Universe; or perhaps the picture of lightning.
X *yin*	酉	*yu*	(ancient form ) vase in which grain is fermented and which will give alcoholic drink.
XI *yang*	戌	*hsü*	(ancient form ) wound from a cutting weapon, idea of destruction: clearing the ground before sowing.
XII *yin*	亥	*hai*	(ancient form ) a man and a woman under a roof, the most propitious time for impregnation.

Chapter 6

Origin of the Cyclic Emblems The Twelve Animals

THE CYCLE OF THE TWELVE ANIMALS

The animals are more popular in China and Vietnam than the duodenary signs or the terrestrial branches with which they are associated. They are certainly better known in the West and numerous works have popularised the horoscopes which can be drawn from them. Besides which, they contain a symbolism which appeals more to the imagination than abstract signs. But this is precisely why more serious interpreters of the signs distrust them and pay them little more than amused attention. If it is necessary not to make too facile a symbolism of the Five Agents, it is all the more dangerous in the case of the Twelve Animals.

The origin of what is sometimes called the Chinese Zodiac is obscure, for no serious comparison with the signs of the Western Zodiac can be drawn. Some have wished to equate them with the names by which the Persians designated the hours, but again, apart from a somewhat similar use of animal's names, no firm conclusion can be made. In fact, the Twelve Animals are essentially linked to the yearly cycle and to the twelve dwellings in Jupiter in its revolution of twelve years.

It is necessary to emphasise that this parallel cycle should not be confused with the Terrestrial Branches because they are not *Yin* or *Yang* in the same way. They are used for the years and hours (more rarely) and never for months and days.

It would seem that far from looking for a foreign source, the origin of their choice should be sought in the treasures of Chinese folklore, for all are heroes of old legends and all are auspicious.[24]

The **RAT** is *yin* for it is a creature of the night. Supposed to live 300 years, it becomes white after its hundredth year. Very auspicious for those who realise that it is a symbol of wealth and prosperity, the rat does not stay in ill-provided houses. It is usefully endowed with second sight.

The **BUFFALO** is born of essence of the thousand year old pine. It is *yin* because the water-buffalo seems to rise out of the soft earth of the paddy field. It helps cultivation and should not be used for butcher's meat (like a horse in the West). A sign of longevity. Lao Tzŭ, the philosopher, rode a buffalo on his journeys among the mountains in his search for immortality. The transcendental buffalo lives for thousands of years.

The **TIGER** is *yang* because it is born in the seventh month, period of the formation of the celestial *yang*. Its stripes are an auspicious mixture of *yin* and *yang*. It is the chief of animals, the terror of demons and ghosts which it devours without pity, and so is charged with the protection of children against evil spirits. Young boys are often dedicated to the tiger and wear a tiger's-head hat to repel jealous spirits which want to suck their souls out of them.

The **HARE** is *yin* because it is formed from the *yin* essence. In its transcendental form it prefers to live in the Moon. It lives for a thousand years and turns white after five hundred years. A wise counsellor by reason of its foresight and ability to make the most of its opportunities.

The **DRAGON** is a *yang* creature and the best of all symbols. (But take care. It is so auspicious that its virtue can be inverted and thereby become dangerous.) It is the king of everything. Symbol of the Emperor, it directs the rains and the clouds. But, above all, when it chooses to live in water it acquires the five colours of dawn and becomes fully beneficent. In a kingdom, the Green Dragon manifests itself when the sovereign is virtuous; contrariwise, its colleague the Blue Dragon, only shows itself when calamities occur. However, if they choose to appear simultaneously it is a symbol of especially good augury. Unhappily the old texts are silent on the signs of these manifestations.

The **SNAKE** is of the same nature as the Dragon *(yang)*. Its presence in the foundations of a dwelling is above all a sign of wealth, if one knows how to 'name' it and if it does not show itself. Its sudden appearance is a warning and a very bad omen.

The **HORSE** is the very symbol of masculinity *(yang)* and is associated with the masculine trigram (p. 13). According to a very ancient tradition, the eight horses are symbols of all the happinesses. It is the image of helpful strength.

The **GOAT** is *yang*, because it shares in the forces of vegetation. Very auspicious, for it is the symbol of social success and a distinguished career.

The **MONKEY** is thought by some to be *yin* and *yang* at one and the same time. It is the symbol of intelligence and resourcefulness, sometimes a touch dishonest. Didn't the Monkey King owe his immortality to the peach he stole from the garden of the Queen of the West? It lives for several thousands of years. In its youth, up to 800 years of age, it is not always benevolent. But it improves with age and when it is transformed into a baboon it becomes charming and helpful.

The **COCK** is *yang* because it is born of Wood exposed to the sun. Its voice rouses and encourages and it chases demons who flee at the sight of its comb (the Chinese believe that red frightens demons).

The **DOG** is *yin*. Although, as food, it is as little appreciated in China as a fricassee of rabbit, it is auspicious, wise and loyal like a sure and useful friend for its flair helps it to spot ambushes and hidden dangers.

The **PIG** is *yin* and the symbol of ease and family prosperity (the ideogram which signifies family represents a pig peacefully installed under a roof). It is a sign of wealth and is always a happy augury, its presence attracts happiness and good fortune.

As with the animals, such as eagles, sheep and bees of Western iconography, one can see that these emblems have been chosen because they are auspicious and should not be interpreted in too naturalistic a way. They bear the mark of strong Taoist influence.

It should be noted that the Vietnamese have replaced the hare with the cat. The people of the Far East consider the hare to be impure and inedible, but we must not confuse substitutions of this sort with the accusations sometimes made against low eating houses. Let us just bear in mind that in the popular speech of North China the word 'rabbit' is regarded as an insult and that in its stead a less ill-sounding word, wild cat, is used. The substitution of cat for rabbit in Vietnam has perhaps a similar origin.

Chapter 7

The Five Agents
Wood, Fire, Earth, Metal, Water

THE MANIFESTATION OF ENERGY: THE FIVE AGENTS

At first energy manifests itself by the opposition of *Yin* and *Yang*. In a second stage energy is subdivided into five forces (or rather 4 + 1, Earth being primarily a point of reference which is identified with the centre). The study of the five forces illustrates perfectly the inconvenience, to which I have referred, of trying to interpret in a Western way concepts which are purely Chinese.

The term 行 *Hsing*, which I have translated as 'Agent', means in Chinese 'to march, progress'. It is thus essentially dynamic and denotes the future. However, the sinologues, impressed no doubt by Empedocles' vision of the world which reduced the components of everything to four fundamental elements: Water, Air, Earth and Fire, united by love and separated by hate, insist on translating *Hsing* as 'element'. Apart from giving a contrary meaning, this translation is wrong in suggesting that the combination of these five 'elements', Metal, Wood, Water, Fire and Earth, forms the substance of all things.

In fact, and Chinese tradition is unanimous on this point, it is concerned only with symbols, well chosen too, which represent the forces animating the universe; ancient images, moreover, whose usefulness has been demonstrated by experience. We should remember all that has been said above about *Yin* and *Yang*.

Out of respect for the tradition established by his brother sinologues, Needham preserves the word 'element', but he deprives it of all meaning in indicating that it is not concerned with elements belonging to the constitution of things but with 'processes',[25] that is to say, if I am not mistaken, with principles of evolution or the constant change of all matter.

Thus the Agent which I might call the 'virtue of Water' represents an infiltrating and dissolving action which sinks downwards; the 'virtue of Fire' a boiling hot action rising upwards; the 'virtue of Wood' is alive and accepts the form given it by a tool; while the 'virtue of Metal' is inert but embraces the shape imposed on it by the mould; the 'virtue of Earth' is distinct from the others since they are all derived from it. Of course, these descriptions should not be taken literally; and a reality should not be attributed to what are merely symbols.

Jacques Lavier, who of all French acupuncturists seems to me to be the one most in sympathy with Chinese mentality and texts, has given an excellent explanation taken from the *Nei Ching* which I reproduce here. Having established that these are concerned above all with energy, he has chosen to translate them as the 'five potentials' and describes their action thus: Fire, connected with Summer and the South, symbolises the 'great *Yang*' in its extreme sense, while Water, connected with Winter and the North, symbolises the 'great *Yin*'. Wood, connected with Spring and the East, is the 'little *Yin*', the diminishing *Yin* which loses strength in contrast with the dynamic *Yang* which grows like vegetation. Metal is the 'little *Yang*', the *Yang* which regresses and is connected with the Autumn and the West. *Yang* will give way to a destructive *Yin*. Earth, being situated in the Centre, is in direct relation with the other 'potentials', all of which, in fact, it contains.[26]

This traditional explanation has the advantage of showing better the relationships between the Five Agents, a translation decidedly preferable to 'potential' which seems to me to suggest a force which is merely latent. Let us emphasise, nevertheless, that according to the tradition followed by all acupuncturists, Lavier is referring to a cosmic astrology applied to the whole Universe. The astrology which is concerned with the destiny of each one of us in particular is a little different, for, in this perspective, each Agent, as we shall see, is alternately an expanding *yang* or a receptive *yin*.

AFFINITIES AND RELATIONSHIPS OF THE FIVE AGENTS

Over the centuries, astrologers and acupuncturists have established catalogues of beings or of states which seemed to have privileged relationships with one or another of the Five Agents. One could make an endless list of them; but, apart from the fact that they are linked to traditions both diverse and often contradictory which can interest only the curious and the erudite, the esoteric nature of some catalogues would necessitate long and difficult explanations. I prefer to content myself with a combination of the lists in the *Nei Ching* and the *Yüeh Ling*.

The EAST in the sky produces the wind which expresses itself on earth[27] by the Agent Wood whose season is the Spring: WOOD rules the *liver*, the eyes, the muscles. Its colour is green, its taste acid, nourishment suitable to it is mutton and corn. Planet Jupiter. Number 8 (numerical symbol).

The SOUTH in the sky produces heat which expresses itself on earth by the Agent Fire whose season is the Summer: FIRE rules the *heart*, the tongue, blood. Its colour is red, its taste bitter, nourishment suitable to it is chicken and peas. Planet Mars. Number 7.

The CENTRE in the sky produces humidity which expresses itself on earth by the Agent Earth, whose season is the Dog Days: EARTH rules the *spleen*, the mouth and flesh. Its colour is yellow, its taste is sweet and sugary, nourishment suitable to it is beef and millet. Planet Saturn. Number 5.

The WEST in the sky produces aridity which expresses itself on earth by the Agent Metal, whose season is the Autumn: METAL rules the *lungs*, the nose, the skin and hair. Its colour is white, its taste pungent, nourishment suitable to it is dog and oily grains. Planet Venus. Number 9.

The NORTH in the sky produces cold which expresses itself on Earth by the Agent Water, whose season is the Winter: WATER rules the *kidneys*, the ears and bones. Its colour is black, its taste salty, nourishment suitable to it is pork and sorghum. Planet Mercury. Number 6.

THE ASSOCIATION OF THE FIVE AGENTS AND YIN AND YANG IN THE EVOLUTION OF TIME

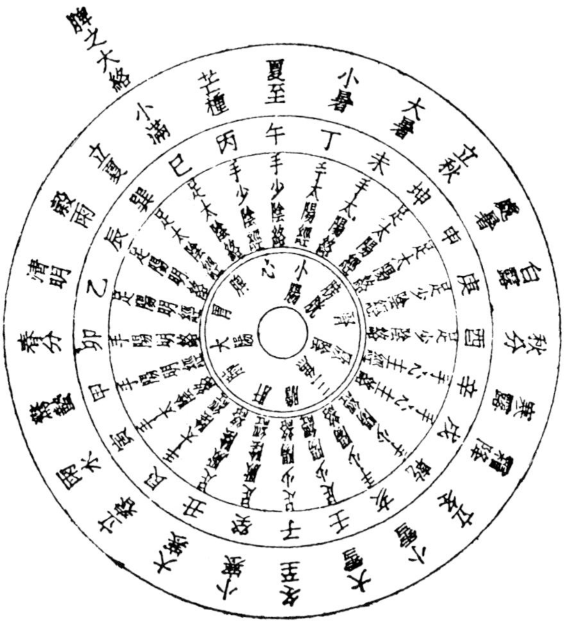
夏至
小暑
芒種
丙
午
丁
未
坤
申
庚
酉
辛
巳
辰
乙
卯
甲

Diagram taken from the *Nan Ching*. In the outer circle the twenty-four solar terms, in the next the cyclic characters, then the meridians (lines connecting points in acupuncture), and in the centre the organs concerned.[28]

Chinese Seasons and months follow an identical rhythm, similar in some respects to a biorhythm. The seasons begin a month and a half before Western Seasons. The Winter solstice, Spring equinox, Summer solstice and Autumn equinox come in the middle and are the peaks of their respective seasons. In a similar way, the twelve Chinese astrological periods start fifteen days before the beginning of the Western Zodiac signs, at the climax therefore and not at the beginning of the Chinese astrological months. Although each sign of the Zodiac and each Chinese astrological period measures 30° of the ecliptic, they are nevertheless unequal in time for the solar Winter mansions are shorter than the Summer ones. The full strength, therefore, of a season, a month and even an hour, is always in the middle, as it is with the moon in a lunar month.

The Five Agents have an influence all through the year but each of them except for Earth has a maximum and a minimum. According to the *Nèi Ching*, Wood's maximum is in the Spring equinox, and its minimum at the time of the Autumn equinox. Metal's maximum is in the Autumn equinox, and minimum in the Spring equinox. In the same way, Fire's maximum is in the Summer solstice and its minimum in the Winter solstice; and Water's maximum is in the Winter solstice and its minimum is in the Summer solstice.[29]

Earth follows a different course and appears in its greatest strength at the last month of each season indicating a return to the Centre.

The following chart illustrates what we have just said:

THE FIVE AGENTS AND THE FOUR SEASONS

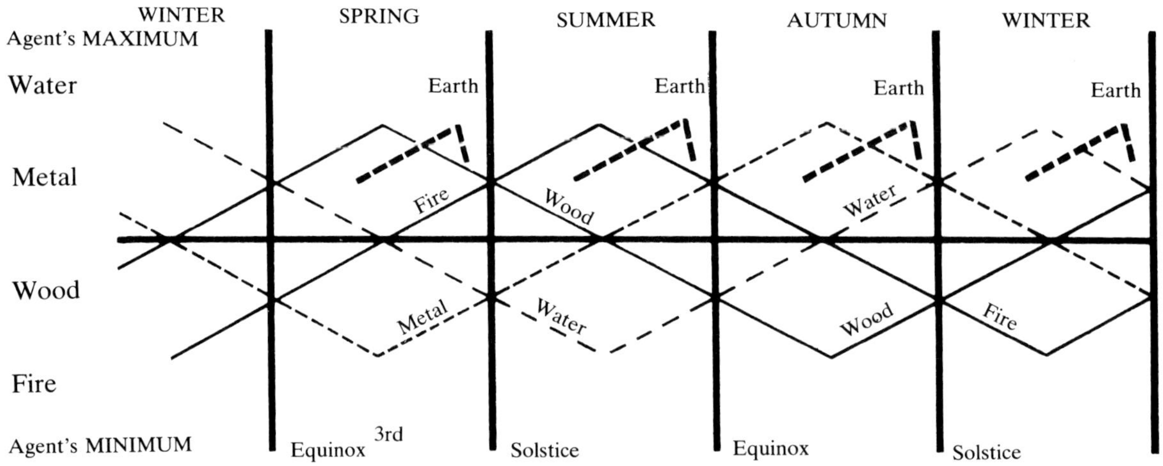
WINTER
SPRING
SUMMER
AUTUMN
WINTER
Agent's MAXIMUM
Water
Earth
Earth
Earth
Earth
Metal
Fire
Wood
Water
Wood
Metal
Water
Wood
Fire
Fire
Agent's MINIMUM
Equinox
3rd
Solstice
Equinox
Solstice

THE FIVE AGENTS AND THE MONTHS

The chart below shows the combination of the foregoing with the appearance of *yin* and *yang* during the year.

ALTERNATION OF YIN AND YANG DURING THE YEAR

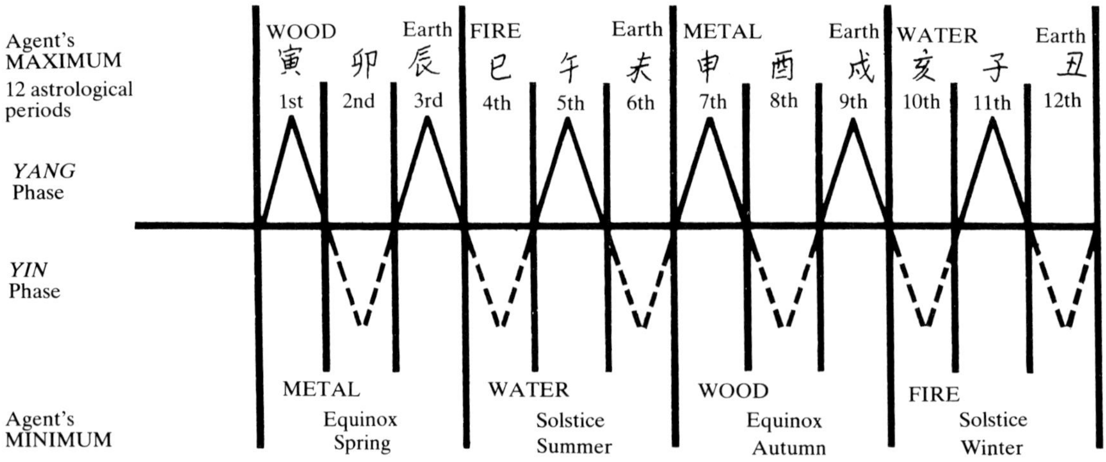
Agent's MAXIMUM
12 astrological periods
YANG Phase
YIN Phase
Agent's MINIMUM
WOOD
Earth
FIRE
Earth
METAL
Earth
WATER
Earth
寅 卯 辰 巳 午 未 申 酉 戌 亥 子 丑
1st 2nd 3rd 4th 5th 6th 7th 8th 9th 10th 11th 12th
METAL
Equinox
Spring
WATER
Solstice
Summer
WOOD
Equinox
Autumn
FIRE
Solstice
Winter

Following the rule of odd and even numbers, we see that the 2nd month (Spring equinox) is *yin*; the 5th month (Summer solstice) is *yang*; the 8th month (Autumn equinox) is *yin*; the 11th month (Winter solstice) is *yang*. But the 5th and 11th months are called '*yang* between two *yin*'; this partly explains an extraordinary statement made by some esoteric authors that the signs of the 5th and 11th months are *yin*.

THE FIVE AGENTS AND THE DAY

The hours go the same way as the months, but as the duodenary signs appear in a different order so also do the Agents.

ALTERNATION OF YIN AND YANG DURING THE DAY

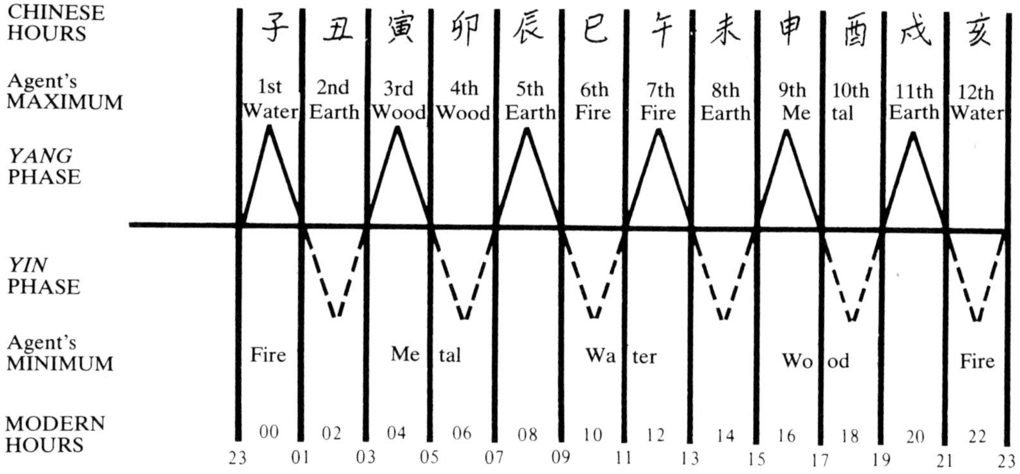
CHINESE HOURS
子 丑 寅 卯 辰 巳 午 未 申 酉 戌 亥
Agent's MAXIMUM
1st Water
2nd Earth
3rd Wood
4th Wood
5th Earth
6th Fire
7th Fire
8th Earth
9th Me
10th tal
11th Earth
12th Water
YANG PHASE
YIN PHASE
Agent's MINIMUM
Fire
Me tal
Wa ter
Wo od
Fire
MODERN HOURS
00 02 04 06 08 10 12 14 16 18 20 22
23 01 03 05 07 09 11 13 15 17 19 21 23

The above charts show that the interplay of *yin* and *yang* and the Five Agents is not as simple as it may seem.

It is well worth pondering on these charts before beginning any interpretation of the four pillars or eight signs of a person's destiny.

N.B. All that we have said above applies to both lunar and solar calendars.

THE AGENTS AND THE SECRET SOCIETIES

I recently came across an interesting document which shows how members of Chinese secret societies use the Five Agents to indicate the relationships between different members. Metal means the Head and Water the brotherhood.

金
木
土
火
水

Our illustration shows the gestures which indicates the five actions. From left to right Metal, Wood, Earth, Fire and Water.[30]

AFFINITIES OF THE FIVE AGENTS

Agents	*Wood*	*Fire*	*Earth*	*Metal*	*Water*
Points of compass	East	South	Centre	West	North
Seasons	Spring	Summer	Dog Days	Autumn	Winter
Denary signs	1, 2	3, 4	5, 6	7, 8	9, 10
Duodenary signs	III, IV	VI, VII	II, V, VIII, IX	IX, X	XII, I
Planets	Jupiter	Mars	Saturn	Venus	Mercury
Organs	Liver	Heart	Spleen	Lungs	Kidneys
Flavours	Acid	Bitter	Sweet	Acrid	Salty
Numbers	8	7	5	9	6
Notes of pentatonic scale	ch'iao 3rd note	ch'eng 4th note	kung 1st note	shang 2nd note	yü 5th note
Colours	green	red	yellow	white	black
Style of government	relaxed	enlightened	prudent	energetic	calm
Virtues	benevolence	wisdom	faith	rectitude	respectability
Emotional states	anger	joy	desire	sadness	fear

The list contained in this table could be continued indefinitely and Chinese commentators have not hesitated to do so, but I have thought it best to confine it to those terms which are useful to our purpose: thus terms such as 'style of government', 'virtues', etc., can easily be transposed in the course of a study of character.

Chapter 8

The Twenty-Eight Constellations

THE TWENTY-EIGHT CONSTELLATIONS, LUNAR DWELLINGS, OR THE LUNAR ZODIAC

These twenty-eight constellations, symbols of the lunar month, are strictly speaking the only astrological element in the Chinese horoscope. They form a cycle of twenty-eight days which move in parallel with the sexagenary cycle. The constellations (associated with the Agent which rules your group of daily signs of destiny) determine the factor of chance attached to each one of us. Chinese almanacs take care to show them against each day for it is these which indicate above all the activities which are forbidden or recommended for the day.

Here is the list of these constellations as given by Havret, with one or two amendments. Needham thinks that they correspond to the equator as it was in 2400 BC.[31]

Astronomy has always been practised in China for the purpose of defining the temporal order. Here two experts, following a very ancient method, are calculating the equinox of spring with the help of a gnomon.

EASTERN CONSTELLATIONS
Green Dragon Sector

Name	*Symbolic animal*	*Equatorial extension*	*Determining star, right ascension*	*Quality*
1. *Horn*	Crocodile	11° 49′ 48″	α of Virgo 13 h 19 min 55 sec	auspicious
2. *Neck*	Dragon	8° 52′ 12″	ϰ of Virgo 14 h 07 min 34 sec	inauspicious
3. *Root*	Badger	14° 46′ 48″	α^2 of Libra 14 h 45 min 21 sec	inauspicious
4. *Room*	Hare	4° 55′ 48″	π of Scorpio 15 h 52 min 48 sec	auspicious
5. *Heart*	Fox	4° 55′ 48″	σ of Scorpio 16 h 15 min 07 sec	auspicious
6. *Tail*	Tiger	17° 44′ 24″	μ^1 of Scorpio 16 h 45 min 06 sec	auspicious
7. *Basket*	Leopard	11° 00′ 00″	γ of Sagittarius 17 h 59 min 23 sec	auspicious

NORTHERN CONSTELLATIONS
Black Turtle Sector

Name	Symbolic animal	Equatorial extension	Determining star, right ascension	Quality
8. *Ladle*	Unicorn	25° 48′	φ of Sagittarius 18 h 39 min 25 sec	auspicious
9. *Buffalo*	Buffalo	7° 53′ 24″	β of Capricorn 20 h 15 min 24 sec	inauspicious
10. *Woman*	Bat	11° 49′ 48″	σ of Aquarius 20 h 42 min 16 sec	inauspicious
11. *Void*	Rat	9° 51′ 36″	β of Aquarius 21 h 26 min 18 sec	inauspicious
12. *Roof*	Swallow	16° 45′ 36″	α of Aquarius 22 h 00 min 39 sec	inauspicious
13. *House*	Pig	15° 46′ 12″	α of Pegasus 22 h 59 min 47 sec	auspicious
14. *Wall*	Porcupine	8° 52′ 12″	γ of Pegasus 00 h 08 min 05 sec	auspicious

WESTERN CONSTELLATIONS
White Tiger Sector

Name	Symbolic animal	Equatorial extension	Determining star, right ascension	Quality
15. *Legs*	Wolf	15° 46′ 12″	η of Andromeda 00 h 42 min 02 sec	inauspicious
16. *Link*	Dog	11° 49′ 48″	β of Aries 01 h 49 min 07 sec	auspicious
17. *Stomach*	Pheasant	13° 48′	41 of Aries 02 h 44 min 06 sec	auspicious
18. *Lights*	Cock	10° 50′ 24″	η of Taurus 03 h 41 min 32 sec	inauspicious
19. *Thread*	Crow	15° 46′ 12″	ε of Taurus 04 h 22 min 47 sec	auspicious
20. *Turtle*	Monkey	1° 58′ 12″	λ of Orion 05 h 29 min 38 sec	inauspicious
21. *Three associates*	Gibbon	8° 52′ 12″	ζ of Orion 05 h 35 min 43 sec	auspicious

SOUTHERN CONSTELLATIONS
Vermilion Bird Sector

Name	Symbolic animal	Equatorial extension	Determining star, right ascension	Quality
22. *Well*	Tapir	32° 31′ 48″	μ of Gemini 06 h 16 min 55 sec	auspicious
23. *Ghost*	Goat	3° 56′ 24″	θ of Cancer 08 h 25 min 54 sec	inauspicious
24. *Willow*	Buck	14° 46′ 48″	δ of Hydra 08 h 32 min 22 sec	inauspicious
25. *Star*	Horse	6° 54′ 00″	α of Hydra 09 h 22 min 40 sec	inauspicious
26. *Square fishing net*	Stag	17° 44′ 24″	μ of Hydra 10 h 21 min 15 sec	auspicious
27. *Wings*	Snake	17° 44′ 24″	α of Crater 10 h 54 min 54 sec	inauspicious
28. *Chariot*	Earthworms	16° 45′ 36″	γ of Corvus 12 h 10 min 40 sec	auspicious

STARS COMPOSING THESE TWENTY-EIGHT CONSTELLATIONS

1 α and ζ of Virgo.
2 κ ι φ λ of Virgo.
3 α^2 ι^1 γ β of Libra
4 π ρ δ β of Scorpio.
5 σ α τ of Scorpio.
6 μ ε ξ η θ ι κ λ υ of Scorpio.
7 γ δ ε β of Sagittarius.

8 φ λ μ^1 σ τ ζ of Sagittarius.
9 β α^2 ξ^2 π ο ρ of Capricorn.
10 ε^2 and μ of Aquarius.
11 β of Aquarius and α of Equuleus.
12 α of Aquarius, θ and ε of Pegasus.
13 α and β of Pegasus.
14 γ of Pegasus and α of Andromeda.

15 η ζ ι ε δ π ν μ β of Andromeda, σ^2 of Pisces, as well as eleven other stars of these two Constellations.
16 β γ α of Aries.
17 35, 39, 41 of Aries.
18 17, 16, 19, 20, 12, η, 28, 27 of Taurus: the Pleiades.
19 ζ δ^3 δ^1 γ α θ^1, 71, λ of Taurus: Aldebaran and the Hyades.
20 λ φ^1 φ^2 of Orion.
21 ζ ε δ α γ κ β of Orion.

22 μ ν γ ξ δ ε ζ λ of Gemini.
23 θ η γ δ of Cancer.
24 δ σ η ρ ε ζ ω θ of Hydra.
25 α τ^1 τ^2 ι, 27 of Hydra.
26 ν^1 λ μ of Hydra.
27 α γ ζ λ ν η δ ι κ ε of Crater, as well as ten other stars of Crater and of Hydra.
28 γ ε δ β of Corvus.

THE TWENTY-EIGHT CONSTELLATIONS AND THE DAYS OF THE WEEK

This division of time into periods of twenty-eight days corresponds with four weeks: 7×4. It is clear that each constellation will return regularly on the same day of the week. The practice of referring to periods of seven days in Chinese calendars dates from the seventh century AD when Nestorian Christian communities, from Persia, began to have some influence in China.

It is not, therefore, just a matter of chance that the 'Seven Luminaries' are found in the Chinese almanacs: the Sun, the Moon and the five planets, associated with the constellations in exactly the same way as our days of the week. Thus, the constellations

1, 8, 15, 22,	associated with	木星	Jupiter	return on Thursday
2, 9, 16, 23,	associated with	金星	Venus	return on Friday
3, 10, 17, 24,	associated with	土星	Saturn	return on Saturday
4, 11, 18, 25,	associated with	日	Sun	return on Sunday
5, 12, 19, 26,	associated with	月	Moon	return on Monday
6, 13, 20, 27,	associated with	火星	Mars	return on Tuesday
7, 14, 21, 28,	associated with	水星	Mercury	return on Wednesday

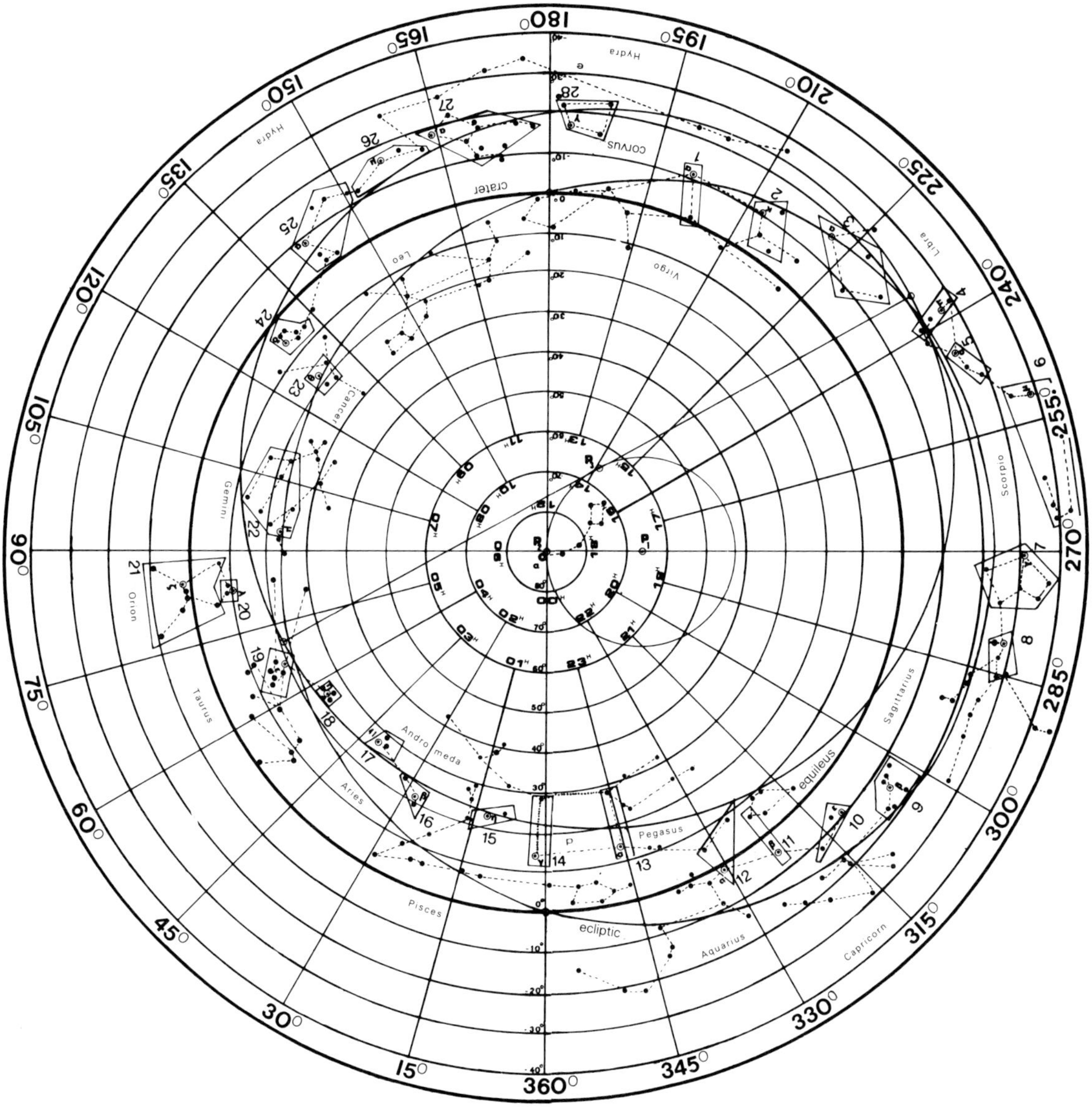

180°
165°
195°
150°
210°
135°
225°
120°
240°
105°
255°
90°
270°
75°
285°
60°
300°
45°
315°
30°
330°
15°
345°
360°
Hydra
Corvus
crater
Leo
Virgo
Libra
Cancer
Gemini
Scorpio
Orion
Taurus
Andromeda
Aries
Pegasus
equileus
Sagittarius
Pisces
ecliptic
Aquarius
Capricorn

The twenty-eight constellations, lunar dwellings, compared with the Western Zodiac.

Although the names of the five Planets (in this list of the seven Luminaries) refer to the Agents with which they are related (for example, Jupiter with Wood, Venus with Metal, etc.), Chinese astrologers have never taken this fact into account. Moreover, when the Chinese wish to refer to the days of the week, which is a concept imported by the Christians, they number the days and do not use the names of the seven Luminaries.[32]

Chapter 9

Relationships between the Eight Signs of Destiny and Numerology, the I Ching and Geomancy. Recapitulary table

1 NUMEROLOGY

Given the capital importance which the early Chinese accorded to music, and the intensive study they made of the mathematical relationships between the musical scales and the length of bamboo tubing which defined them, it is not surprising that they developed a system similar to that of Pythagoras, attributing to numbers a primordial importance in the comprehension of the Universe. One significant distinction, however, is that the Pythagoreans, having a more metaphysical mind, considered numbers to be constitutional elements of the Universe, while the Chinese saw in them merely numerical signs whose function was to represent the Universe and which constituted the sole means of measuring it and thus controlling it.

(a) The magical squares

Thus, because he had had the revelation of the two magical squares, the mythical Emperor *Yü* the Great was able to survey and take possession of the World. His rôle of Supreme Chief of Weights and Measures had the same magical importance for the Emperor as that of defining the calendar. According to tradition, *Yü* himself 'by his voice, his height and his step was able to serve as the standard for all measurement.'[33]

Although they have to some extent fallen out of use, these squares were held in high regard in antiquity, and are still well respected by the Taoist tradition.

The first square, *Ho T'u* the 'Chart of the Yellow River', was transmitted to the Emperor *Yü* by a dragon issuing from the Yellow River. This diagram, made up of rows of black dots (*yin* numbers) and white dots (*yang* numbers), bears symbolically all the figures representing

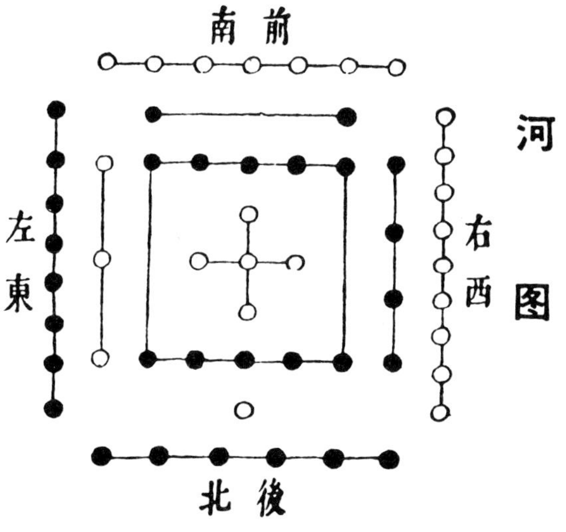
南 前
河 图
左 東
右 西
北 後

The *Ho T'u*

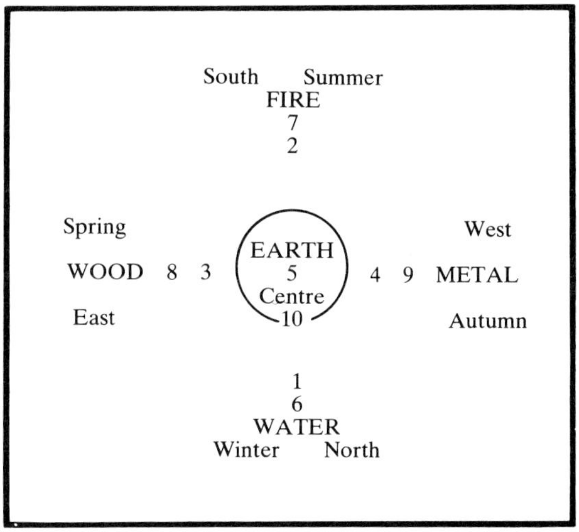
South Summer
FIRE
7
2
Spring
WOOD 8 3
East
EARTH
5
Centre
10
4 9 METAL
West
Autumn
1
6
WATER
Winter North

Key to the interpretation of the *Ho T'u*

the points of the compass, the seasons and the Five Agents: everything in fact which is needed to define space–time relationships.

The second magical square, *Lo Shu* the 'Writing of the River *Lo*', is even better known than the first. It appeared to the Emperor *Yü* inscribed on the back of a tortoise. (The tortoise, with its round back representing Heaven and its flat belly representing Earth, is the symbol of the Universe). The nine prime numbers are arranged in a magical square and were, in early times, represented by nine ritual cauldrons. This arrangement in the form of a square was used to divide the fields (paddy fields) for cultivation, when it was necessary to share them out, and for the palace of the Emperor, the *Ming T'ang*.

It is easy to see that the numbers arranged thus always total fifteen, whether they are read horizontally, vertically or diagonally.

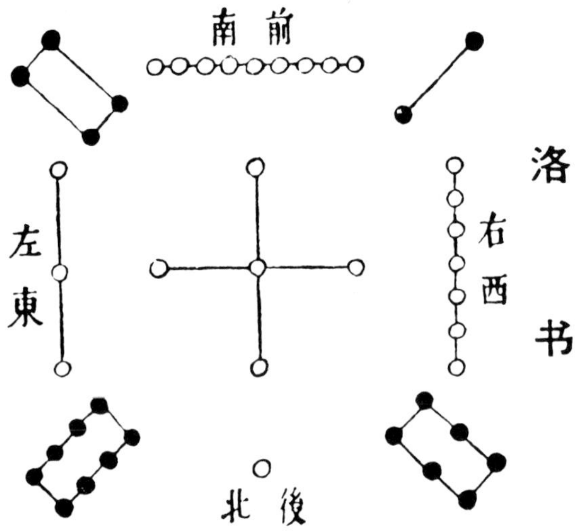
南 前
左
東
右
西
洛
书
北 後

4	9	2
3	5	7
8	1	6

The *Lo Shu*

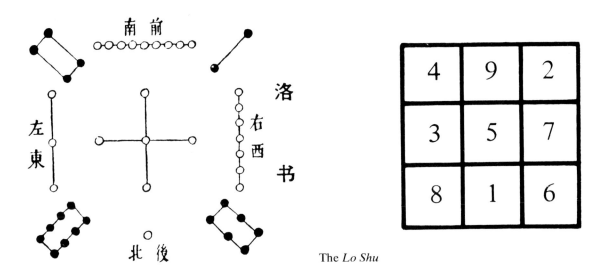

As Granet has noted, the Chinese make no distinction between cardinal and ordinal numbers.[34] We have seen the importance of calculations in the establishment of a horoscope, one might therefore reduce a horoscope to simple numerical relationships and some astrologers have indeed done so. Although I have met experts in this system, I must confess that these mathematical jugglings are a bit beyond me and I have been unable so far to find a serious explanation of it in any work of divination, except in almanacs and then only in a very simplistic form. In effect, to each binomial is attributed a number called 'weight' for convenience. The total weight obtained is thought to indicate the value ascribed by fate to an individual destiny. In short, this is a popular form of numerology.

(b) The Five Agents and Numerology

It is not without interest to note here that in the *Hong Fang*, which contains one of the oldest known lists of the Five Agents, their order is given thus:

WATER	FIRE	WOOD	METAL	EARTH
1	2	3	4	5

According to all traditions, these are also their numerical value and, be it noted, total 15.

Since it specialises in the calendar, the *Yüeh Ling* is concerned only with the higher numbers of the pairs given in the *Ho T'u*: 1–6, 2–7, 3–8, 4–9, which in turn give:

WATER	FIRE	WOOD	METAL
6	7	8	9

totalling 30 (the number of the days of the month). Note that we find the same numbers if we add 5 to each of the numbers of the preceding list.

If we regroup the Agents in the order of production used in this work, we have WOOD = 8, FIRE = 7: Spring, Summer, the waxing period of the Year totalling 15; and METAL = 9, WATER = 6, the declining period of the Year, totalling 15. This applies equally in the daily cycle to the two periods: midnight-midday waxing and midday-midnight declining.

One may also note that 8 & 7 correspond respectively with the dynamic young *yin* & young *yang* – waxing period – while 6 & 9 correspond with the old *yin* & old *yang* in their plenitude, but which are considered by the *I Ching* to be approaching their decline.

2 THE *I CHING*

Most Chinese astrologers use, in conjunction with the Eight Signs, the 64 hexagrams of the *I Ching*, 'the Book of Changes'. The 64 hexagrams represent all the possible combinations of the 8 trigrams which themselves represent all possible combinations of the two principles of *Yin* and *Yang*. We have already seen an illustration of the 8 linked trigrams in the Taoist symbol of the Universe on page 13.[35]

(a) The *I Ching* & Numerology

According to Chinese historians, these trigrams would have been directly inspired by the magic square, *Lo Shu*, of which we have just been speaking. How this could be is not very clear! Many Chinese historians affirm, therefore, that the secret of the true interpretation of the eight trigrams is now lost and with it the secret of the meaning of the sixty-four hexagrams which are derived from them.

This is not the place to describe the *I Ching* method of telling fortunes. There are many books on this subject several of which are excellent. Let us confine ourselves to one interesting aspect.

If we remember that *Yang* is odd and *Yin* even, and that, in order to discover a particular hexagram, *Yang* is given the value 3 and *Yin* the value 2, each line, found by three casts of sticks (or coins) may be thought of as waxing or 'young' or as declining or 'old'.

The dynamic 'young *Yang*' will be symbolised by 7 (2 + 2 + 3) with 2 *Yin* aspects for 1 *Yang* aspect; and the dynamic 'young *Yin*' will be symbolised by 8 (3 + 3 + 2) with 2 *Yang* aspects for 1 *Yin* aspect.

The moving 'old *Yang*', having reached the perfection which will make it change its sign, has the value 9 (3 + 3 + 3) or 3 *Yang* aspects; while the moving 'old *Yin*' has the value 6 (2 + 2 + 2) or 3 *Yin* aspects. According to the *I Ching* method of divination, the 'moving' lines will change to their opposites: an 'old *Yang*' will become 'young *Yin*' and an 'old *Yin*' a 'young *Yang*'.

This is the key to all divination by the *I Ching* where every hexagram containing moving lines engenders another hexagram; and it is this transformation which is significant: the

'Book of Changes' is based on that which evolves and not on that which is static. In any case, the parallel between the lines composing the hexagrams and the Agents is very suggestive and worth thinking about.

(b) The *I Ching* and the Calendar

It is not surprising that a concordance between the hexagrams and the twelve months of the year should be perceived. Here is the best known table:

SEASONS	WINTER			SPRING			SUMMER			AUTUMN		
MONTHS	10th	11th	12th	1st	2nd	3rd	4th	5th	6th	7th	8th	9th
	— —	— —	— —	— —	— —	— —	———	———	———	———	———	———
	— —	— —	— —	— —	— —	———	———	———	———	———	———	— —
	— —	— —	— —	— —	———	———	———	———	———	———	— —	— —
	— —	— —	— —	———	———	———	———	———	———	— —	— —	— —
	— —	— —	———	———	———	———	———	———	— —	— —	— —	— —
Serial numbers	— —	———	———	———	———	———	———	— —	— —	— —	— —	— —
of hexagrams:	2	24	19	11	34	43	1	44	33	12	20	23

Some authors go so far as to identify each hexagram with a precise period of the year. Here is the interpretation given by Blofeld who uses the lunar calendar.[36] [If, however, we were to use astrological periods, the result would be even more satisfactory.]

'The following table gives a list of the . . . months with which each of the hexagrams has a special correspondence. However, it should not be understood that anything forecast by a particular hexagram will certainly occur in that part of the year to which it is related, unless the text expressly indicates this. On the other hand, if we put to the *I Ching* the question "in which month will so and so happen?" the answer will be found in this table.'

First period:

— —	— —	— —	———	— —	———
— —	———	———	— —	— —	— —
— —	— —	———	———	———	— —
———	———	— —	— —	— —	———
———	———	— —	— —	———	— —
———	———	———	— —	— —	— —
11	5	17	35	40	52

Second period:

— —	— —	———	———	— —
— —	— —	———	— —	———
———	———	———	— —	———
———	— —	— —	———	— —
———	— —	———	———	— —
———	— —	— —	— —	— —
34	16	6	18	45

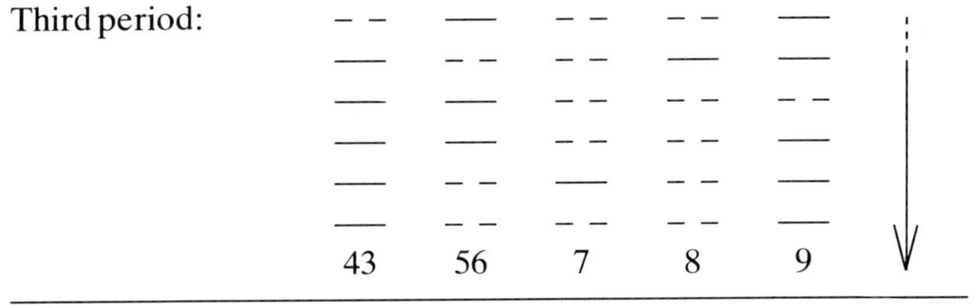
Third period:
43 56 7 8 9

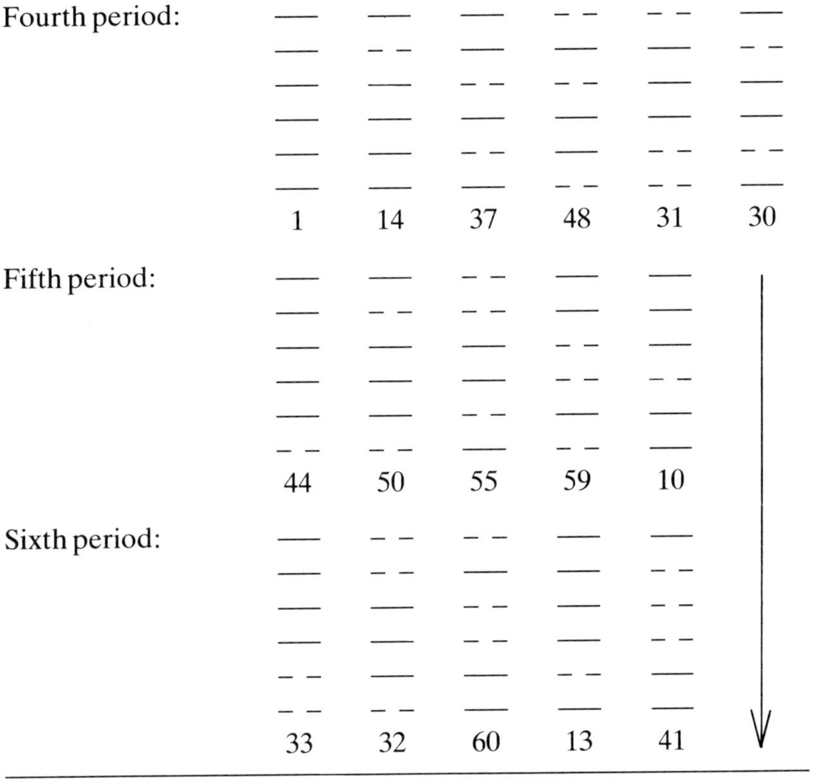
Fourth period:
1 14 37 48 31 30
Fifth period:
44 50 55 59 10
Sixth period:
33 32 60 13 41

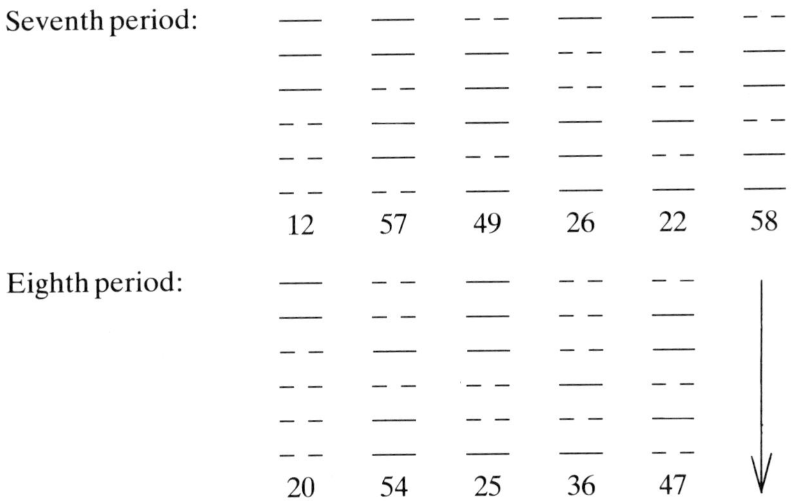
Seventh period:
12 57 49 26 22 58
Eighth period:
20 54 25 36 47

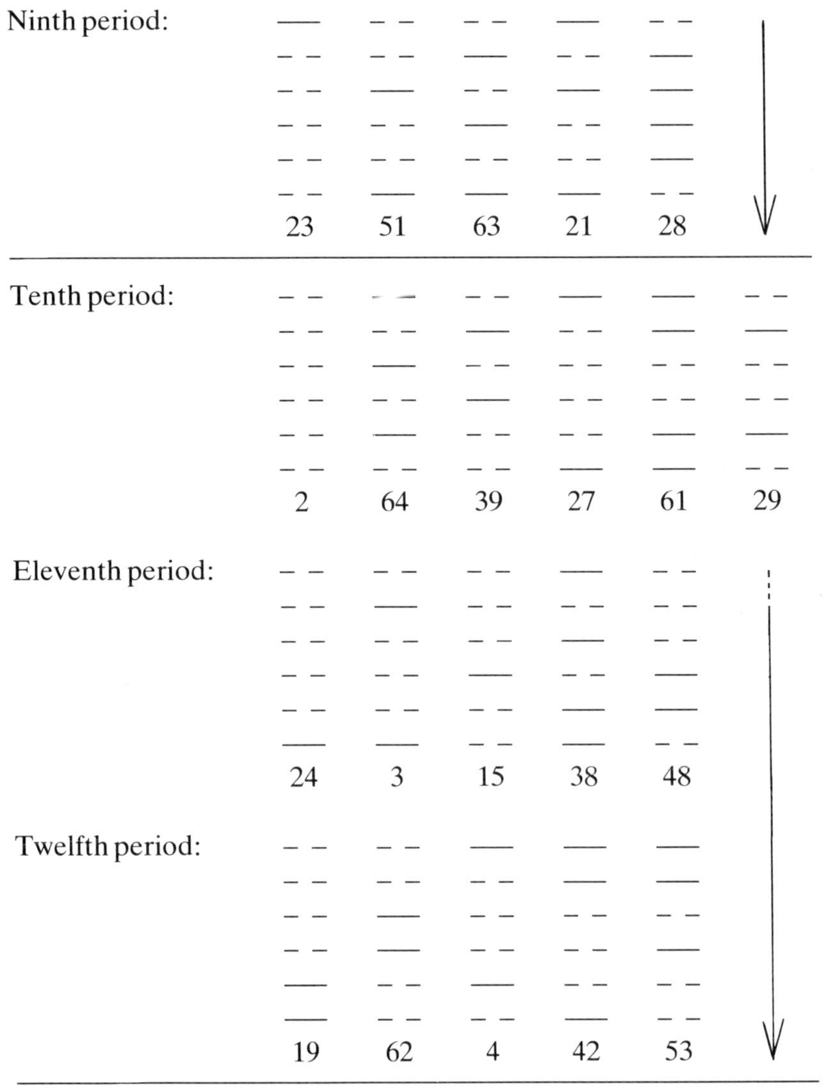
Ninth period:
23 51 63 21 28
Tenth period:
2 64 39 27 61 29
Eleventh period:
24 3 15 38 48
Twelfth period:
19 62 4 42 53

(To find the correspondence of the periods with the Western calendar see page 68.)

'. . . each hexagram governs six particular days. Furthermore, each line of that hexagram will be found to govern one of those six days. Thus a moving line four in hexagram 5 would indicate the tenth day of the first month; a moving line six in hexagram 53 would indicate the last day of the twelfth month and so on. It will be noticed that four of the hexagrams govern a whole three month period each. This table and means of reckoning is based upon an elaborate circular diagram attributed to the legendary Emperor *Fu Hsi* . . .'

3 THE GEOMANTIC COMPASS

As is well known, the Chinese used the compass less for navigation than for defining on the ground the points of the compass and auspicious and inauspicious influences by a system imaginatively called *Feng Shui* (Wind and Water). The basis of calculation is essentially the same as that used for the calendar and the establishment of a horoscope.

For the Chinese, Space and Time are not distinct notions but two aspects of the same and indivisible reality. Ecologists without knowing it, they have always sought to place a building, a house or pavilion, according to the points of the compass and beneficent influences, with the admirable result that the structure is perfectly adapted to the site and the surrounding country. Peking shares with Versailles the privilege of having been planned entirely in conformity with the directives of astrologers and geomanticians.

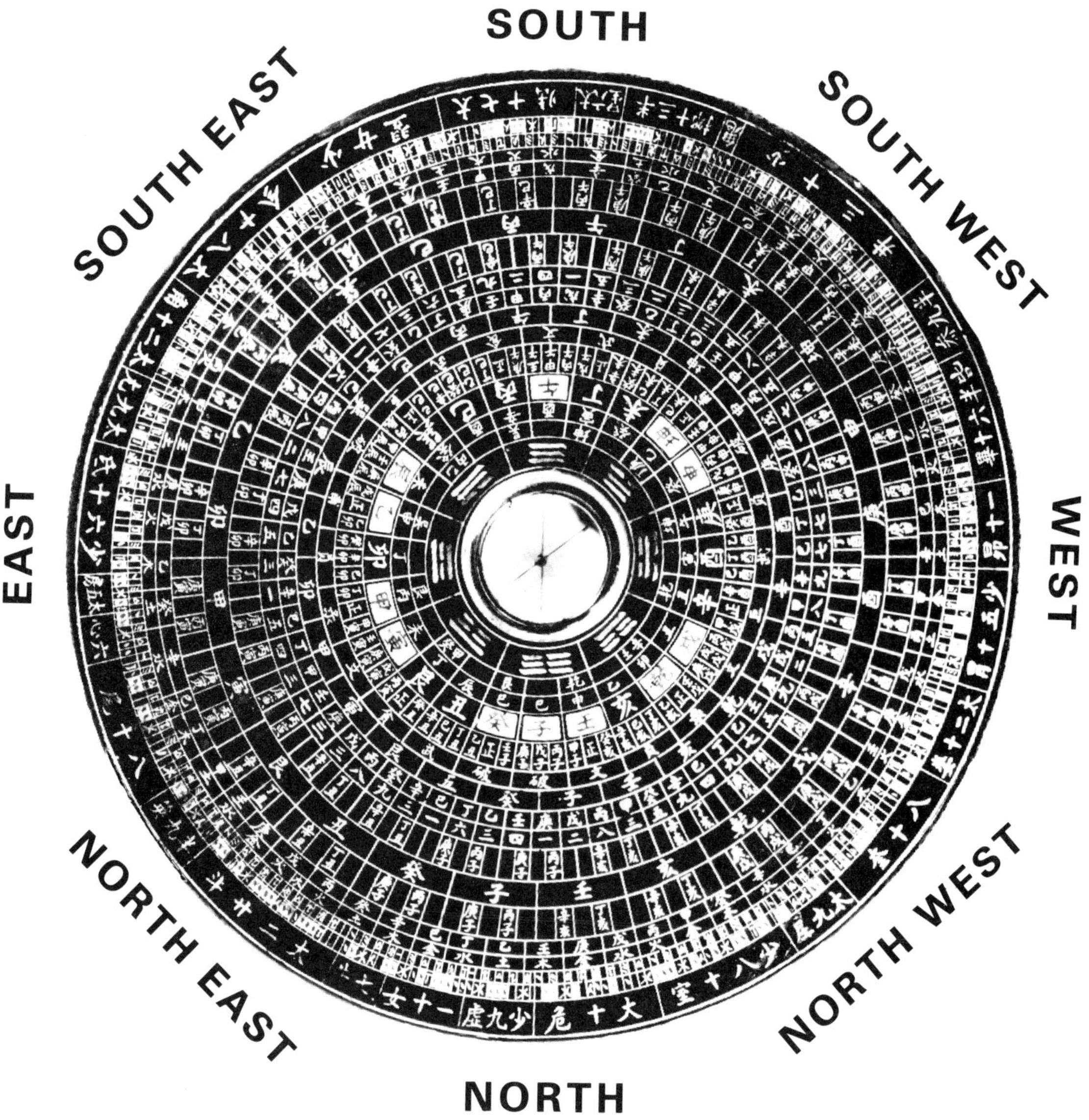
SOUTH
SOUTH WEST
WEST
NORTH WEST
NORTH
NORTH EAST
EAST
SOUTH EAST

GEOMANTIC COMPASS

From his tomb a deceased person continues to watch over his family; and so the choice of its site and orientation is still the subject of detailed study by geomantic experts.

The tool for all these calculations is the geomantic compass which is placed in several circles containing the same data used in horoscopes. In the beautiful and very elaborate compass shown above, we find moving from the outside inwards, the twenty-eight constellations, the prime numbers (in abridged form) and then a complicated melange of binomials, cyclic characters separately mixed with the names of the trigrams, the Five Agents, and near the centre another series of cyclic characters linked to the cardinal points. Next to the centre of the compass are the trigrams themselves representing the eight principal directions. It should be noted that the compass in China is supposed to indicate the South. For this reason we have placed South at the top, North at the bottom, East to the left and West to the right, as we have done consistently throughout this book.[37]

4 RECAPITULARY TABLE SHOWING THE RELATIONSHIPS BETWEEN THE COSMIC CYCLE AND THE ASTROLOGICAL CALENDAR USED IN THIS BOOK

The Cosmic Cycle, which for the Chinese governs the relationships between Heaven and Earth and thus the Universal Order, is quite different from that used for genthliacal astrology, the science of individual horoscopes. Nevertheless, this cycle is very important if one wishes to study the influences which govern the evolution of the World and which will therefore react on our own destiny. It is the same in acupuncture for the 'Twelve Meridians' mark on our bodies (as their Chinese denominations prove) the cosmic influences to which all individuals are subject.[38]

The cosmic cycle is ruled by the sexagenary cycle already known to us:

Celestial influences are linked to the figure 6, and thus (by an inversion which we have already emphasised) to the Twelve Terrestrial Branches, and are manifested by the 'Six Energies' (known sometimes as the 3 *Yang* and the 3 *Yin*) which are, in order, the lesser *Yin*, the extreme *Yin*, the lesser *Yang*, the middle *Yang*, the extreme *Yang* and the middle *Yin*. They are associated in this order with the first six terrestrial branches, and then, in turn and in the same order, with the last six. They are also associated with the Five Agents; but, in order to allow the relationship to be established in a consistent manner, FIRE is divided into two called respectively 'ministerial Fire and imperial Fire'.

Terrestrial influences are linked to the figure 5 and thus to the Ten Celestial Stems. They are manifested by the 'Five Movements' denoting in this case the Five Agents but grouped in an order quite different from that we have used up to now. Seasonal cycles, constituted on the same principles, revolve within this annual cycle and justify the complex variation of the seasons in spite of their originally simple scheme.

It is not possible here to give more details of the cosmic cycle beyond these brief ideas which, nevertheless, will allow each one of us to confront his own destiny with the general outline for each year. All that is necessary is to apply the rules which we know already about the relationships between the Five Agents.

Explanation of the Recapitulatory Table

In the middle we find three cycles of 60 Years (for more details about those cycles see page 23): the past from 1864 to 1923 (2nd in the series of three); the present from 1924 to 1983 (3rd in the series of three); the future from 1984 to 2043 (1st in a new series of three). In the bottom left hand corner of each rectangle a figure indicates the number of the binomial of each year.

1st The Cosmic Cycle

A. The Cosmic Cycle and the Six Movements: – signifies lesser; = signifies middle; + signifies extreme (in relationship with the Branches).

B. The Agents in relationship with the Five Movements. M.F. Ministerial Fire; I.F. Imperial Fire (in relationship with the Branches).

C. The Five Movements or the Five Agents in relationship with the Cosmic Order (in relationship with the Stems).

2nd The Astrological Cycle

D. The Five Agents in relationship with the Duodenary Cycle (Twelve Terrestrial Branches).

E. The Twelve Terrestrial Branches.

F. The Five Agents considered in their relationship with the Denary Cycle (Ten Celestial Stems).

G. The Ten Celestial Stems.

H. The cycle of Twelve Animals in relationship with the Duodenary Cycle.

3rd Applications

I. The series of Twelve Chinese hours.

J. The Twelve monthly periods of the astrological cycle.

A COSMIC CYCLE			少陰 YIN –	太陰 YIN +	少陽 YANG –	陽明 YANG =	太陽 YANG +	厥陰 YIN =	少陰 YIN –	太陰 YIN +	少陽 YANG –	陽明 YANG =	太陽 YANG +	厥陰 YIN =
B '6' Agents			相火 M.F.	土 E	君火 I.F.	金 M	水 Wr	木 Wd	相火 M.F.	土 E	君火 I.F.	金 M	水 Wr	木 Wd
	D		水 Wr	土 E	木 Wd	木 Wd	土 E	火 F	火 F	土 E	金 M	金 M	土 E	水 Wr
C Cosmic	F	E G	子 I	丑 II	寅 III	卯 IV	辰 V	巳 VI	午 VII	未 VIII	申 IX	酉 X	戌 XI	亥 XII
土 Earth	木 Wd	甲 1	1864 **1924** 1984 1		1914 **1974** 2034 51		1904 **1964** 2024 41		1894 **1954** 2014 31		1884 **1944** 2004 21		1874 **1934** 1994 11	
金 Metal	木 Wd	乙 2		1865 **1925** 1985 2		1915 **1975** 2035 52		1905 **1965** 2025 42		1895 **1955** 2015 32		1885 **1945** 2005 22		1875 **1935** 1995 12
水 Water	火 F	丙 3	1876 **1936** 1996 13		1866 **1926** 1986 3		1916 **1976** 2036 53		1906 **1966** 2026 43		1896 **1956** 2016 33		1886 **1946** 2006 23	
木 Wood	火 F	丁 4		1877 **1937** 1997 14		1867 **1927** 1987 4		1917 **1977** 2037 54		1907 **1967** 2027 44		1897 **1957** 2017 34		1887 **1947** 2007 24
火 Fire	水 E	戊 5	1888 **1948** 2008 25		1878 **1938** 1998 15		1868 **1928** 1988 5		1918 **1978** 2038 55		1908 **1968** 2028 45		1898 **1958** 2018 35	

土 Earth	水 E	巳 6		1889 **1949** 2009 26		1879 **1939** 1999 16		1869 **1929** 1989 6		1919 **1979** 2039 56		1909 **1969** 2029 46		1899 **1959** 2019 36
金 Metal	金 M	庚 7	1900 **1960** 2020 37		1890 **1950** 2010 27		1880 **1940** 2000 17		1870 **1930** 1990 7		1920 **1980** 2040 57		1910 **1970** 2030 47	
水 Water	金 M	辛 8		1901 **1961** 2021 38		1891 **1951** 2011 28		1881 **1941** 2001 18		1871 **1931** 1991 8		1921 **1981** 2041 58		1911 **1971** 2031 48
木 Wood	水 Wr	壬 9	1912 **1972** 2032 49		1902 **1962** 2022 39		1892 **1952** 2012 29		1882 **1942** 2002 19		1872 **1932** 1992 9		1922 **1982** 2042 59	
火 Fire	水 Wr	癸 10		1913 **1973** 2033 50		1903 **1963** 2023 40		1893 **1953** 2013 30		1883 **1943** 2003 20		1873 **1933** 1993 10		1923 **1983** 2043 60
		H	鼠 Rat	牛 Buffalo	虎 Tiger	兔 Hare	龍 Dragon	蛇 Snake	馬 Horse	羊 Goat	猴 Monkey	雞 Cock	犬 Dog	猪 Pig
		I	23 — 01	01 — 03	03 — 05	05 — 07	07 — 09	09 — 11	11 — 13	13 — 15	15 — 17	17 — 19	19 — 21	21 — 23
		J	11th M	12th M	1st M	2nd M	3rd M	4th M	5th M	6th M	7th M	8th M	9th M	10th M

亥
辰
寅
丑
戌
子
酉
申
未
巳
午
卯

Part II

THE MAKING OF A HOROSCOPE

The Green Dragon, symbol of the East and of the *Yang* principle, bearing the 12 duodenary signs (the Terrestrial Branches): the 1st on the mouth, the 2nd on the neck, the 3rd on the middle of the tail, the 4th on the left front paw, the 5th on the right, the 6th on the left rear paw, the 7th on the right, the 8th 9th 10th on the body from left to right, the 11th on the beginning of the tail, the 12th on the end of the tail.

Chapter 10

How to cast a Horoscope

THE ESTABLISHMENT OF THE ASTROLOGICAL THEME

Time in China is defined by the combination of two parallel cycles of ideograms: one of ten ideograms or denary; the other of twelve ideograms or duodenary. Groups of two ideograms, one from each of these cycles, are the basis of Chinese astrology. They are names which give a kind of personality to each year, each month, each day and each hour. For convenience we will, from now on, term each group binomials. The maximum number of combinations of binomials is sixty and these themselves form a cycle known as the Sexagenary Cycle.[39]. Sixty is thus the essential number on which all calculations for converting the Western calendar to the Chinese system are based.

Each binomial is numbered from one to sixty, and for practical reasons it will be more convenient to call them by those numbers when establishing the astrological theme, rather than using the ideograms themselves. The binomials are used in the same cyclic manner for the year: a cycle of sixty years; for the month: a cycle of five years; for the day: a cycle of sixty days; and for the hour: a cycle of five days. (Remember that the Chinese day was traditionally divided into twelve periods of two hours each.)

Note that the binomials, as well as their two elements, are *Yang* when the number is odd and *Yin* when it is even. The significance of *Yin* and *Yang* has already been discussed.[40]

To establish a horoscope, therefore, it is sufficient to know the serial numbers of the binomials representing the year, the month, the day and the hour of one's birth. These binomials contain the eight signs of your destiny.

To find them we must now carry out four operations: one for each of the four relevant binomials whose serial numbers constitute a sort of code, which give the key to our character and temperament and which, in a sense, might be described as the cards dealt to us at birth.

1 How to calculate the binomial for the year of birth

There are two ways of calculating the year (and the month as you will see later on):

(a) The best known method is based on the lunar calendar. In this case the year begins with the Chinese New Year which falls on a date varying between 21 January and 20 February (both dates inclusive). See tables on pages 64 to 67.

(b) The other method is the one preferred by Chinese astrologers[41] who reckon the beginning of the astrological year to be the solar date for the 'establishment of Spring', which falls on 4 or 5 February. For greater precision see the tables on pages 68 to 71 which show the exact time for the establishment of spring for each year of the twentieth century.

I agree with the Chinese astrologers and propose to use the solar calendar for my calculations. It is important, therefore, to remember that for this purpose 1950, for example, ran from 4 February 1950 to 3 February 1951.

Once you are sure of the beginning, Chinese fashion, of the year of birth, nothing is more easy than finding the binomial of the year to which you belong. To convert the year of the Christian era to the Chinese system take 3 from the number of the Western year then divide by 60; the remainder (or 60) indicates the number of the binomial you are looking for.

Example: for someone born on 19 August 1912, the binomial of the year will be: $1912-3=1909$, divided by 60, the remainder is 49. 49 is the number of the binomial.

2 How to calculate the binomial of the month of birth

As for the year there are two possible methods:
(a) One is to follow the lunar calendar which is preferred by the Vietnamese and many Chinese. In this case the Chinese year comprises twelve or thirteen moons (lunar months) of twenty-nine or thirty days. Thus the year comprises 354 or 355 days. Seven times in nineteen years an intercalary moon is added in the same way that an extra day is added to a leap year in the West. This intercalary moon has no personality of its own; instead, it is called by the same name as the preceding moon which it duplicates. For this reason you will see in the table that certain moons are doubled: for example, the 6th moon of 1911 or the 5th moon of 1914.

The cycle of sixty binomials lasts five years. Since, astrologically, the Winter solstice traditionally falls in the first moon of the cycle, the first moon of the following year comes two months later and is therefore identified as the third binomial. At the same time, the two last moons of the cycle will be known by the names of the first and second binomials.
(b) The other method which is thought to be more logical by Chinese astrologers is to take the twelve periods defined by the twelve solar terms which fall midway between the Western signs of the Zodiac. These periods are stable and each represents 30° of the 360° of the Zodiac (see tables on pages 68–71).

In both cases, the cycle of 60 months is the same and the way to find the binomial of the month of a person's birth is thus very simple:

remember that in those years ending in	*the first month is known by the name of*
4 or 9	the 3rd binomial
5 or 0	the 15th binomial
6 or 1	the 27th binomial
7 or 2	the 39th binomial
8 or 3	the 51st binomial

Now turn to the following tables to see how they work by taking the same example of a person born on 19 August 1912:
(a) If you are following the lunar calendar, look at the table on page 64 and you will find that the 7th moon begins on 13 August.
(b) If you prefer the solar calendar, you will find in the table on page 68 that the 7th period of the year begins on 8 August.

In both cases the number of the binomial of the month is the same. The binomial of the month will be different only for people born between 8 and 12 August inclusive.

EXPLANATORY NOTES TO THE TABLES

1 Tables of concordance between the Universal Calendar and the Lunar Calendar

These tables show all the lunations which occur from 1900 to 1999. An intercalary month does not have its own signs: it duplicates the preceding month and has the same serial numbers and signs. To avoid confusion we use the letter L (lunation) to indicate the month of the lunar calendar.[42]

In each column the first number indicates the day, and the second the month, of the Western calendar in which the lunation begins. Those who prefer to use the Astrological Calendar can find the phases of the moon for a given day in these tables.

The first line at the top of the table shows the usual Chinese names for the months (in numerical order). The second line shows the duodenary sign attributed to each month. The names in Chinese of the seasons whose culminating points are the equinoxes and solstices are shown at the bottom of each page. In the Lunar Calendar, they coincide only approximately with each period of three months.

2 Tables of concordance between the Universal Calendar and the Chinese Astrological Calendar

The Chinese Astrological Calendar is based on the 24 solar terms. Odd-numbered terms indicate the beginning of each of the twelve periods, and even-numbered terms the culminating point which coincides exactly with the signs of the Western Zodiac (for the complete list of the solar terms see page 20). All Chinese almanacs show the exact hour at which each of the terms begins. Since we do not possess a complete collection of almanacs since 1900, we have to calculate the mean time to the nearest 0 or 5 (as Western astrologers usually do for the signs of the Zodiac). The given time is that of Peking. It is necessary to subtract eight hours for GMT.[42]

The Chinese names of the astrological months are shown in the first line at the top of the page with the names of their approximately equivalent months in English underneath. The duodenary signs are in the third line. The letter P indicates the astrological period.

In succeeding lines, the first number of each box is the day of the month when the astrological period begins. The second, smaller number, indicates the time.

In the Astrological Calendar the Chinese seasons, shown at the bottom of each page, coincide exactly with each series of three periods of astrological months.

LUNAR–SOLAR CALENDAR (1)

UNIVERSAL CALENDAR	正月 寅 III 1 L	二月 卯 IV 2 L	三月 辰 V 3 L	四月 巳 VI 4 L	五月 午 VII 5 L	六月 未 VIII 6 L	七月 申 IX 7 L	八月 酉 X 8 L	九月 戌 XI 9 L	十月 亥 XII 10 L	十一月 子 I 11 L	十二月 丑 II 12 L
1900	31 **1**	1 **3**	31 **3**	29 **4**	28 **5**	27 **6**	26 **7**	25 **8**; 24 **9**	23 **10**	22 **11**	22 **12**	20 **1**
1901	19 **2**	20 **3**	19 **4**	18 **5**	16 **6**	16 **7**	14 **8**	13 **9**	12 **10**	11 **11**	11 **12**	10 **1**
1902	8 **2**	10 **3**	8 **4**	8 **5**	6 **6**	5 **7**	4 **8**	2 **9**	2 **10**	31 **10**	30 **11**	30 **12**
1903	29 **1**	27 **2**	29 **3**	27 **4**	27 **5**; 25 **6**	24 **7**	23 **8**	21 **9**	20 **10**	19 **11**	19 **12**	17 **1**
1904	16 **2**	17 **3**	16 **4**	15 **5**	14 **6**	13 **7**	11 **8**	10 **9**	9 **10**	7 **11**	7 **12**	6 **1**
1905	4 **2**	6 **3**	5 **4**	4 **5**	3 **6**	3 **7**	1 **8**	30 **8**	29 **9**	28 **10**	27 **11**	26 **12**
1906	25 **1**	23 **2**	25 **3**	24 **4**; 23 **5**	22 **6**	21 **7**	20 **8**	18 **9**	18 **10**	16 **11**	16 **12**	14 **1**
1907	13 **2**	14 **3**	13 **4**	12 **5**	11 **6**	10 **7**	9 **8**	8 **9**	7 **10**	6 **11**	5 **12**	4 **1**
1908	2 **2**	3 **3**	1 **4**	30 **4**	30 **5**	29 **6**	28 **7**	27 **8**	25 **9**	25 **10**	24 **11**	23 **12**
1909	22 **1**	20 **2**; 22 **3**	20 **4**	19 **5**	18 **6**	17 **7**	16 **8**	14 **9**	14 **10**	13 **11**	13 **12**	11 **1**
1910	10 **2**	11 **3**	10 **4**	9 **5**	7 **6**	7 **7**	5 **8**	4 **9**	3 **10**	2 **11**	2 **12**	1 **1**
1911	30 **1**	1 **3**	30 **3**	29 **4**	28 **5**	26 **6**; 26 **7**	24 **8**	22 **9**	22 **10**	21 **11**	20 **12**	19 **1**
1912	18 **2**	19 **3**	17 **4**	17 **5**	15 **6**	14 **7**	13 **8**	11 **9**	1 **10**	9 **11**	9 **12**	7 **1**
1913	6 **2**	8 **3**	7 **4**	6 **5**	5 **6**	4 **7**	2 **8**	1 **9**	30 **9**	29 **10**	28 **11**	27 **12**
1914	26 **1**	25 **2**	27 **3**	25 **4**	25 **5**; 23 **6**	23 **7**	21 **8**	20 **9**	19 **10**	17 **11**	17 **12**	15 **1**
1915	14 **2**	16 **3**	14 **4**	14 **5**	13 **6**	12 **7**	11 **8**	9 **9**	9 **10**	7 **11**	7 **12**	5 **1**
1916	3 **2**	4 **3**	3 **4**	2 **5**	1 **6**	30 **6**	30 **7**	29 **8**	27 **9**	27 **10**	25 **11**	25 **12**
1917	23 **1**	22 **2**; 23 **3**	21 **4**	21 **5**	19 **6**	19 **7**	18 **8**	16 **9**	16 **10**	15 **11**	14 **12**	13 **1**
1918	11 **2**	13 **3**	11 **4**	10 **5**	9 **6**	8 **7**	7 **8**	5 **9**	5 **10**	4 **11**	3 **12**	2 **1**
1919	1 **2**	2 **3**	1 **4**	30 **4**	29 **5**	28 **6**	27 **7**; 25 **8**	24 **9**	24 **10**	22 **11**	22 **12**	21 **1**

1920	20 2	20 3	19 4	18 5	16 6	16 7	14 8	12 9	12 10	10 11	10 12	9 1
1921	8 2	10 3	8 4	8 5	6 6	5 7	4 8	2 9	1 10	31 10	29 11	29 12
1922	28 1	27 2	28 3	27 4	27 5 / 25 6	24 7	23 8	21 9	20 10	19 11	18 12	17 1
1923	16 2	17 3	16 4	16 5	14 6	14 7	12 8	11 9	10 10	8 11	8 12	6 1
1924	5 2	5 3	4 4	4 5	2 6	2 7	1 8	30 8	29 9	28 10	27 11	26 12
1925	24 1	23 2	24 3	23 4 / 22 5	21 6	21 7	19 8	18 9	18 10	16 11	16 12	14 1
1926	13 2	14 3	12 4	12 5	10 6	10 7	8 8	7 9	7 10	5 11	5 12	4 1
1927	2 2	4 3	2 4	1 5	31 5	29 6	29 7	27 8	26 9	25 10	24 11	24 12
1928	23 1	21 2 / 22 3	20 4	19 5	18 6	17 7	15 8	14 9	13 10	12 11	12 12	11 1
1929	10 2	11 3	10 4	9 5	7 6	7 7	5 8	3 9	3 10	1 11	1 12	31 12
1930	30 1	28 2	30 3	29 4	28 5	26 6 / 26 7	24 8	22 9	22 10	20 11	20 12	19 1
1931	17 2	19 3	18 4	17 5	16 6	15 7	14 8	12 9	11 10	10 11	9 12	8 1
1932	6 2	7 3	6 4	6 5	4 6	4 7	2 8	1 9	30 9	29 10	28 11	27 12
1933	26 1	24 2	26 3	25 4	24 5 / 23 6	22 7	21 8	20 9	19 10	18 11	17 12	15 1
1934	14 2	15 3	14 4	13 5	12 6	12 7	10 8	9 9	8 10	7 11	7 12	5 1
1935	4 2	5 3	3 4	3 5	1 6	1 7	30 7	29 8	28 9	27 10	26 11	26 12
1936	24 1	23 2	23 3 / 21 4	21 5	19 6	18 7	17 8	16 9	15 10	14 11	14 12	13 1
1937	11 2	13 3	11 4	10 5	9 6	8 7	6 8	5 9	4 10	3 11	3 12	2 1
1938	31 1	2 3	1 4	30 4	29 5	28 6	27 7 / 25 8	24 9	23 10	22 11	22 12	20 1
1939	19 2	21 3	20 4	19 5	17 6	17 7	15 8	13 9	13 10	11 11	11 12	9 1
1940	8 2	9 3	8 4	7 5	6 6	5 7	4 8	2 9	1 10	31 10	29 11	29 12
1941	27 1	26 2	28 3	26 4	26 5	25 6 / 24 7	23 8	21 9	20 10	19 11	18 12	17 1
1942	15 2	17 3	15 4	15 5	14 6	13 7	12 8	10 9	10 10	8 11	8 12	6 1
1943	5 2	6 3	5 4	4 5	3 6	2 7	1 8	31 8	29 9	29 10	27 11	27 12
1944	25 1	24 2	24 3	23 4 / 22 5	21 6	20 7	19 8	17 9	17 10	16 11	15 12	14 1
1945	13 2	14 3	12 4	12 5	10 6	9 7	8 8	6 9	6 10	5 11	5 12	3 1
1946	2 2	4 3	2 4	1 5	31 5	29 6	28 7	27 8	25 9	25 10	24 11	23 12
1947	22 1	21 2 / 23 3	21 4	20 5	19 6	18 7	16 8	15 9	14 10	13 11	12 12	11 1
1948	10 2	11 3	9 4	9 5	7 6	7 7	5 8	3 9	3 10	1 11	1 12	30 12
1949	29 1	28 2	29 3	28 4	28 5	26 6	26 7 / 24 8	22 9	22 10	20 11	20 12	18 1
公元	SPRING 春分 EQUINOX			SUMMER 夏至 SOLSTICE			AUTUMN 秋分 EQUINOX			WINTER 冬至 SOLSTICE		

LUNAR–SOLAR CALENDAR (2)

UNIVERSAI CALENDAR	正 月 寅 III 1 L	二 月 卯 IV 2 L	三 月 辰 V 3 L	四 月 巳 VI 4 L	五 月 午 VII 5 L	六 月 未 VIII 6 L	七 月 申 IX 7 L	八 月 酉 X 8 L	九 月 戌 XI 9 L	十 月 亥 XII 10 L	十一月 子 I 11 L	十二月 丑 II 12 L
1950	17 **2**	18 **3**	17 **4**	17 **5**	15 **6**	15 **7**	14 **8**	12 **9**	11 **10**	10 **11**	9 **12**	8 **1**
1951	6 **2**	8 **3**	6 **4**	6 **5**	5 **6**	4 **7**	3 **8**	1 **9**	1 **10**	30 **10**	29 **11**	28 **12**
1952	27 **1**	25 **2**	26 **3**	24 **4**	24 **5** / 22 **6**	22 **7**	20 **8**	19 **9**	19 **10**	17 **11**	17 **12**	15 **1**
1953	14 **2**	15 **3**	14 **4**	13 **5**	11 **6**	11 **7**	9 **8**	8 **9**	8 **10**	7 **11**	6 **12**	5 **1**
1954	3 **2**	5 **3**	3 **4**	3 **5**	1 **6**	30 **6**	30 **7**	28 **8**	27 **9**	27 **10**	25 **11**	25 **12**
1955	24 **1**	22 **2**	24 **3** / 22 **4**	22 **5**	20 **6**	19 **7**	18 **8**	16 **9**	16 **10**	14 **11**	14 **12**	13 **1**
1956	12 **2**	12 **3**	11 **4**	10 **5**	9 **6**	8 **7**	6 **8**	5 **9**	4 **10**	3 **11**	2 **12**	1 **1**
1957	31 **1**	2 **3**	31 **3**	30 **4**	29 **5**	28 **6**	27 **7**	25 **8** / 24 **9**	23 **10**	22 **11**	21 **12**	20 **1**
1958	18 **2**	20 **3**	19 **4**	19 **5**	17 **6**	17 **7**	15 **8**	13 **9**	13 **10**	11 **11**	11 **12**	9 **1**
1959	8 **2**	9 **3**	8 **4**	8 **5**	6 **6**	6 **7**	4 **8**	3 **9**	2 **10**	1 **11**	30 **11**	30 **12**
1960	28 **1**	27 **2**	27 **3**	26 **4**	25 **5**	24 **6** / 24 **7**	22 **8**	21 **9**	20 **10**	19 **11**	18 **12**	17 **1**
1961	15 **2**	17 **3**	15 **4**	15 **5**	13 **6**	13 **7**	11 **8**	10 **9**	10 **10**	2 **11**	8 **12**	6 **1**
1962	5 **2**	6 **3**	5 **4**	4 **5**	2 **6**	2 **7**	31 **7**	30 **8**	29 **9**	28 **10**	27 **11**	27 **12**
1963	25 **1**	24 **2**	25 **3**	24 **4** / 23 **5**	21 **6**	21 **7**	19 **8**	18 **9**	17 **10**	16 **11**	16 **12**	15 **1**
1964	13 **2**	14 **3**	12 **4**	12 **5**	10 **6**	9 **7**	8 **8**	6 **9**	6 **10**	4 **11**	4 **12**	3 **1**
1965	2 **2**	3 **3**	2 **4**	1 **5**	31 **5**	29 **6**	28 **7**	27 **8**	25 **9**	24 **10**	23 **11**	23 **12**
1966	21 **1**	20 **2**	22 **3** / 21 **4**	20 **5**	19 **6**	18 **7**	16 **8**	15 **9**	14 **10**	12 **11**	12 **12**	11 **1**
1967	9 **2**	11 **3**	10 **4**	9 **5**	8 **6**	8 **7**	6 **8**	4 **9**	4 **10**	2 **11**	2 **12**	31 **12**
1968	30 **1**	28 **2**	29 **3**	27 **4**	27 **5**	26 **6**	25 **7** / 24 **8**	22 **9**	22 **10**	20 **11**	20 **12**	18 **1**
1969	17 **2**	18 **3**	17 **4**	16 **5**	15 **6**	14 **7**	13 **8**	12 **9**	11 **10**	10 **11**	9 **12**	8 **1**

1970	6 2	8 3	6 4	5 5	4 6	3 7	2 8	1 9	30 9	30 10	29 11	28 12
1971	27 1	25 2	27 3	25 4	24 5 / 23 6	22 7	21 8	19 9	19 10	18 11	18 12	16 1
1972	15 2	15 3	14 4	13 5	11 6	11 7	9 8	8 9	7 10	6 11	6 12	4 1
1973	3 2	5 3	3 4	3 5	1 6	30 6	30 7	28 8	26 9	26 10	25 11	24 12
1974	23 1	22 2	24 3	22 4 / 22 5	20 6	19 7	18 8	16 9	15 10	14 11	14 12	12 1
1975	11 2	13 3	12 4	11 5	10 6	9 7	7 8	6 9	5 10	3 11	3 12	1 1
1976	31 1	1 3	31 3	29 4	29 5	27 6	27 7	25 8 / 24 9	23 10	21 11	21 12	19 1
1977	18 2	20 3	18 4	18 5	17 6	16 7	15 8	13 9	13 10	11 11	11 12	9 1
1978	7 2	9 3	7 4	7 5	6 6	5 7	4 8	2 9	2 10	1 11	30 11	30 12
1979	28 1	27 2	28 3	26 4	26 5	24 6 / 24 7	23 8	21 9	21 10	20 11	19 12	18 1
1980	16 2	17 3	15 4	14 5	13 6	12 7	11 8	9 9	9 10	8 11	7 12	6 1
1981	5 2	6 3	5 4	4 5	2 6	2 7	31 7	29 8	28 9	28 10	26 11	26 12
1982	25 1	24 2	25 3	24 4 / 23 5	21 6	21 7	19 8	17 9	17 10	15 11	15 12	14 1
1983	13 2	15 3	13 4	13 5	11 6	10 7	9 8	7 9	6 10	5 11	4 12	3 1
1984	2 2	3 3	1 4	1 5	31 5	29 6	28 7	27 8	25 9	24 10 / 23 11	22 12	21 1
1985	20 2	21 3	20 4	20 5	18 6	18 7	16 8	15 9	14 10	12 11	12 12	10 1
1986	9 2	10 3	9 4	9 5	7 6	7 7	6 8	4 9	4 10	2 11	2 12	31 12
1987	29 1	28 2	29 3	28 4	27 5	26 6 / 26 7	24 8	23 9	23 10	21 11	21 12	19 1
1988	17 2	18 3	16 4	16 5	14 6	14 7	12 8	11 9	11 10	9 11	9 12	8 1
1989	6 2	8 3	6 4	5 5	4 6	3 7	1 8	31 8	30 9	29 10	28 11	28 12
1990	27 1	25 2	27 3	25 4	24 5 / 23 6	22 7	20 8	19 9	18 10	17 11	17 12	16 1
1991	15 2	16 3	15 4	14 5	12 6	12 7	10 8	8 9	8 10	6 11	6 12	5 1
1992	4 2	4 3	3 4	3 5	1 6	30 6	30 7	28 8	26 9	26 10	24 11	24 12
1993	23 1	21 2	23 3 / 22 4	21 5	20 6	19 7	18 8	16 9	15 10	14 11	13 12	12 1
1994	10 2	12 3	11 4	11 5	9 6	9 7	7 8	6 9	5 10	3 11	3 12	1 1
1995	31 1	1 3	31 3	30 4	29 5	28 6	27 7	26 8 / 25 9	24 10	22 11	22 12	20 1
1996	19 2	19 3	18 4	17 5	16 6	16 7	14 8	13 9	12 10	11 11	11 12	9 1
1997	7 2	9 3	7 4	7 5	5 6	5 7	3 8	2 9	2 10	31 10	30 11	30 12
1998	28 1	27 2	28 3	26 4	26 5 / 24 6	23 7	22 8	21 9	20 10	19 11	19 12	17 1
1999	16 2	18 3	16 4	15 5	14 6	13 7	11 8	10 9	9 10	8 11	8 12	7 1
公元	SPRING 春分 EQUINOX			SUMMER 夏至 SOLSTICE			AUTUMN 秋分 EQUINOX			WINTER 冬至 SOLSTICE		

ASTROLOGICAL CALENDAR (1)

UNIVERSAL CALENDAR	孟春 FEBRUARY	仲春 MARCH	季春 APRIL	孟夏 MAY	仲夏 JUNE	季夏 JULY	孟秋 AUGUST	仲秋 SEPTEMBER	季秋 OCTOBER	孟冬 NOVEMBER	仲冬 DECEMBER	季冬 JANUARY
	寅 III	卯 IV	辰 V	巳 VI	午 VII	未 VIII	申 IX	酉 X	戌 XI	亥 XII	子 I	丑 II
	1 P	2 P	3 P	4 P	5 P	6 P	7 P	8 P	9 P	10 P	11 P	12 P
1900	4 15h10	6 09h10	5 14h05	6 07h30	6 11h45	7 22h00	8 07h50	8 10h35	9 02h05	8 05h05	7 21h50	6 09h00
1901	4 21h00	6 15h00	5 19h55	6 13h20	6 17h35	8 03h50	8 13h35	8 16h25	9 07h55	8 10h55	8 03h40	6 14h50
1902	5 02h50	6 20h45	6 01h40	6 19h10	6 23h20	8 09h40	8 19h25	8 22h15	9 13h40	8 16h45	8 09h25	6 20h40
1903	5 08h35	7 02h35	6 07h30	7 01h00	7 05h10	8 15h30	9 01h15	9 04h00	9 19h30	8 22h30	8 15h15	7 02h25
1904	5 14h25	6 08h25	5 13h20	6 06h45	6 11h00	7 21h15	8 07h05	8 09h50	9 01h20	8 04h20	7 21h05	6 08h15
1905	4 20h15	6 14h15	5 19h10	6 12h35	6 16h50	8 03h05	8 12h50	8 15h40	9 07h10	8 10h10	8 02h55	6 14h05
1906	5 02h05	6 20h00	6 01h00	6 18h25	6 22h40	8 08h55	8 18h40	8 21h30	9 12h55	8 16h00	8 08h40	6 19h55
1907	5 07h50	7 01h50	6 06h45	7 00h10	7 04h25	8 14h45	9 00h30	9 03h15	9 18h45	8 21h45	8 14h30	7 01h40
1908	5 13h40	6 07h40	5 12h35	6 06h00	6 10h15	7 20h30	8 06h20	8 09h05	9 00h35	8 03h35	7 20h20	6 07h30
1909	4 19h30	6 13h30	5 18h25	6 11h50	6 16h05	8 02h20	8 12h05	8 14h55	9 06h25	8 09h25	8 02h10	6 13h20
1910	5 01h20	6 19h15	6 00h15	6 17h40	6 21h50	8 08h10	8 17h55	8 20h45	9 12h10	8 15h15	8 08h00	6 19h10
1911	5 07h05	7 01h05	6 06h00	6 23h25	7 03h40	8 14h00	8 23h45	9 02h30	9 18h00	8 21h00	8 13h45	7 01h00
1912	5 12h55	6 06h55	5 11h50	6 05h15	6 09h30	7 19h45	8 05h35	8 08h20	8 23h50	8 02h50	7 19h35	6 06h45
1913	4 18h45	6 12h45	5 17h40	6 11h05	6 15h20	8 01h35	8 11h20	8 14h10	9 05h40	8 08h40	8 01h20	6 12h35
1914	5 00h35	6 18h30	5 23h30	6 16h55	6 21h05	8 07h25	8 17h10	8 20h00	9 11h30	8 14h30	8 07h10	6 18h25
1915	5 06h20	7 00h20	6 05h15	6 22h40	7 02h55	8 13h15	8 23h00	9 01h50	9 17h15	8 20h15	8 13h00	7 00h15
1916	5 12h10	6 06h10	5 11h05	6 04h30	6 08h45	7 19h00	8 04h50	8 07h35	8 23h05	8 02h05	7 18h50	6 06h00
1917	4 18h00	6 12h00	5 16h55	6 10h20	6 14h35	8 00h50	8 10h35	8 13h25	9 04h55	8 07h55	8 00h40	6 11h50
1918	4 23h50	6 17h45	5 22h45	6 16h10	6 20h20	8 06h40	8 16h25	8 19h15	9 10h45	8 13h45	8 06h30	6 17h40
1919	5 05h35	6 23h35	6 04h30	6 22h00	7 02h10	8 12h30	8 22h15	9 01h05	9 16h30	8 19h30	8 12h15	6 22h30

1920	5 11h25	6 05h25	5 10h20	6 03h45	6 08h00	7 18h20	8 04h05	8 06h50	8 22h20	8 01h20	7 18h05	6 05h15
1921	4 17h15	6 11h15	5 16h10	6 09h35	6 13h50	8 00h05	8 09h50	8 12h40	9 04h10	8 07h10	7 23h55	6 11h05
1922	4 23h05	6 17h00	5 22h00	6 15h25	6 19h35	8 05h55	8 15h40	8 18h30	9 10h00	8 13h00	8 05h45	6 16h55
1923	5 04h50	6 22h50	6 03h45	6 21h15	7 01h25	8 11h45	8 21h30	9 00h20	9 15h45	8 18h45	8 11h30	6 22h45
1924	5 10h40	6 04h40	5 09h35	6 03h00	6 07h15	7 17h35	8 03h20	8 06h05	8 21h35	8 00h35	7 17h20	6 04h30
1925	4 16h30	6 10h30	5 15h25	6 08h50	6 13h05	7 23h20	8 09h05	8 11h55	9 03h25	8 06h25	7 23h10	6 10h20
1926	4 22h20	6 16h15	5 21h15	6 14h40	6 18h50	8 05h10	8 14h55	8 17h45	9 09h15	8 12h15	8 05h00	6 16h10
1927	5 04h05	6 22h05	6 03h00	6 20h30	7 00h40	8 11h00	8 20h45	8 23h35	9 15h00	8 18h00	8 10h45	6 22h00
1928	5 09h55	6 03h55	5 08h50	6 02h15	6 06h30	7 16h50	8 02h35	8 05h20	8 20h50	7 23h50	7 16h35	6 03h45
1929	4 15h45	6 09h45	5 14h40	6 08h05	6 12h20	7 22h35	8 08h20	8 11h10	9 02h40	8 05h40	7 20h25	6 09h35
1930	4 21h35	6 15h30	5 20h30	6 13h55	6 18h05	8 04h25	8 14h10	8 17h00	9 08h30	8 11h30	8 04h15	6 15h25
1931	5 03h20	6 21h20	6 02h15	6 19h45	6 23h55	8 10h15	8 20h00	8 22h50	9 14h15	8 17h15	8 10h00	6 21h15
1932	5 09h10	6 03h10	5 08h05	6 01h30	6 05h45	7 16h05	8 01h50	8 04h35	8 20h05	7 23h05	7 15h50	6 03h00
1933	4 15h00	6 09h00	5 13h55	6 07h20	6 11h35	7 21h50	8 07h35	8 10h25	9 01h55	8 04h55	7 21h40	6 08h50
1934	4 20h50	6 14h45	5 19h45	6 13h10	6 17h20	8 03h40	8 13h25	8 16h15	9 07h45	8 10h45	8 03h30	6 14h40
1935	5 02h40	6 20h35	6 01h30	6 19h00	6 23h10	8 09h30	8 19h15	8 22h05	9 13h30	8 16h30	8 09h15	6 20h30
1936	5 08h25	6 02h25	5 07h20	6 00h45	6 05h00	7 15h20	8 01h05	8 03h50	8 19h20	7 22h20	7 15h05	6 02h15
1937	4 14h15	6 08h15	5 13h10	6 06h35	6 10h50	7 21h05	8 06h50	8 09h40	9 01h10	8 04h10	7 20h55	6 08h05
1938	4 20h05	6 14h00	5 19h00	6 12h25	6 16h35	8 02h55	8 12h40	8 15h30	9 07h00	8 10h00	8 02h45	6 13h55
1939	5 01h55	6 19h50	6 00h45	6 18h15	6 22h25	8 08h45	8 18h30	8 21h20	9 12h45	8 15h45	8 08h30	6 19h45
1940	5 07h40	6 01h40	5 06h35	6 00h00	6 04h15	7 14h35	8 00h20	8 03h05	8 18h35	7 21h35	7 14h20	6 01h30
1941	4 13h30	6 07h30	5 12h25	6 05h50	6 10h05	7 20h20	8 06h05	8 08h55	9 00h25	8 03h25	7 20h10	6 07h20
1942	4 19h20	6 13h15	5 18h15	6 11h40	6 15h50	8 02h10	8 11h55	8 14h45	9 06h15	8 09h15	8 02h00	6 13h10
1943	5 01h10	6 19h05	6 00h00	6 17h30	6 21h40	8 08h00	8 17h45	8 20h35	9 12h00	8 15h00	8 07h45	6 19h00
1944	5 06h55	6 00h55	5 05h50	5 23h15	6 03h30	7 13h50	7 23h35	8 02h20	8 17h50	7 20h50	7 13h35	6 00h45
1945	4 12h45	6 06h45	5 11h40	6 05h05	6 09h20	7 19h35	8 05h20	8 08h10	8 23h40	8 02h40	7 19h25	6 06h35
1946	4 18h35	6 12h30	5 17h30	6 10h55	6 15h10	8 01h25	8 11h10	8 14h00	9 05h30	8 08h30	8 01h15	6 12h25
1947	5 00h25	6 18h20	5 23h15	6 16h45	6 20h55	8 07h15	8 17h00	8 19h50	9 11h15	8 14h15	8 07h00	6 18h15
1948	5 06h10	6 00h10	5 05h05	5 22h30	6 02h45	7 13h05	7 22h50	8 01h35	8 17h05	7 20h05	7 12h50	6 00h00
1949	4 12h00	6 06h00	5 10h55	6 04h20	6 08h35	7 18h50	8 04h40	8 07h25	8 22h55	8 01h55	7 18h40	6 05h50
公元	春 SPRING			夏 SUMMER			秋 AUTUMN			冬 WINTER		

ASTROLOGICAL CALENDAR (2)

UNIVERSAL CALENDAR	孟春 FEBRUARY	仲春 MARCH	季春 APRIL	孟夏 MAY	仲夏 JUNE	季夏 JULY	孟秋 AUGUST	仲秋 SEPTEMBER	季秋 OCTOBER	孟冬 NOVEMBER	仲冬 DECEMBER	季冬 JANUARY
	寅 III	卯 IV	辰 V	巳 VI	午 VII	未 VIII	申 IX	酉 X	戌 XI	亥 XII	子 I	丑 II
	1 P	2 P	3 P	4 P	5 P	6 P	7 P	8 P	9 P	10 P	11 P	12 P
1950	4 17h50	6 11h45	5 16h45	6 10h10	6 14h25	8 00h40	8 10h25	8 13h15	9 04h45	8 07h45	8 00h30	6 11h40
1951	4 23h40	6 17h35	5 22h30	6 16h00	6 20h10	8 06h30	8 16h15	8 19h05	9 10h30	8 13h30	8 06h15	6 17h30
1952	5 05h25	5 23h25	5 04h20	5 21h45	6 02h00	7 12h20	7 22h05	8 00h50	8 19h20	7 19h20	7 12h05	5 23h15
1953	4 11h15	6 05h15	5 10h10	6 03h35	6 07h50	7 18h05	8 03h55	8 06h40	8 22h10	8 01h10	7 17h55	6 05h05
1954	4 17h05	6 11h00	5 16h00	6 09h25	6 13h40	8 23h55	8 09h40	8 12h30	9 04h00	8 07h00	7 23h45	6 10h55
1955	4 22h55	6 16h50	5 21h45	6 15h15	6 19h25	8 05h45	8 15h30	8 18h20	9 09h45	8 12h50	8 05h30	6 16h45
1956	5 04h40	5 22h40	5 03h35	5 21h00	6 01h15	7 11h35	7 21h20	8 00h05	8 15h35	7 18h35	7 11h20	5 22h30
1957	4 10h30	6 04h30	5 09h25	6 02h50	6 07h05	7 17h20	8 03h10	8 05h55	8 21h25	8 00h25	7 17h10	6 04h20
1958	4 16h20	6 10h15	5 15h15	6 08h40	6 12h55	7 23h10	8 08h55	8 11h45	9 03h15	8 06h15	7 23h00	6 10h10
1959	4 22h10	6 16h05	5 21h00	6 14h30	6 18h40	8 05h00	8 14h45	8 17h35	9 09h00	8 12h05	8 04h45	6 16h00
1960	5 03h55	5 21h55	5 02h50	5 20h15	6 00h30	7 10h50	7 20h35	7 23h20	8 14h50	7 17h50	7 10h35	5 21h45
1961	4 09h45	6 03h45	5 08h40	6 02h05	6 06h20	7 16h35	8 02h25	8 05h10	8 20h40	7 23h40	7 16h25	6 03h35
1962	4 15h35	6 09h30	5 14h30	6 07h55	6 12h10	7 22h25	8 08h10	8 11h00	9 02h30	8 05h30	7 22h15	6 09h25
1963	4 21h25	6 15h20	5 20h15	6 13h45	6 17h55	8 04h15	8 14h00	8 16h50	9 08h15	8 11h20	8 04h00	6 15h15
1964	5 03h10	5 21h10	5 02h05	5 19h30	5 23h45	7 10h05	7 19h50	7 22h40	8 14h05	7 17h05	7 09h50	5 21h00
1965	4 09h00	6 03h00	5 07h55	6 01h20	6 05h35	7 15h50	8 01h40	8 04h25	8 19h55	7 22h55	7 15h40	6 02h50
1966	4 14h50	6 08h45	5 13h45	6 07h10	6 11h25	7 21h40	8 07h25	8 10h15	9 01h45	8 04h45	7 21h30	6 08h40
1967	4 20h40	6 14h35	5 19h30	6 13h00	6 17h10	8 03h30	8 13h15	8 16h05	9 07h30	8 10h35	8 03h15	6 14h30
1968	5 02h25	5 20h25	5 01h20	5 18h45	5 23h00	7 09h20	7 19h05	7 21h55	8 13h20	7 16h20	7 09h05	5 20h15
1969	4 08h15	6 02h15	5 07h10	6 00h35	6 04h50	7 15h05	8 00h55	8 03h40	8 19h10	7 22h10	7 14h55	6 02h05

1970	4 14h05	6 08h00	5 13h00	6 06h25	6 10h40	7 20h55	8 06h40	8 09h30	9 01h00	8 04h00	7 20h45	6 07h55
1971	4 19h55	6 13h50	5 18h45	6 12h15	6 16h25	8 02h45	8 12h30	8 15h20	9 06h45	8 09h50	8 02h30	6 13h45
1972	5 01h40	5 19h40	5 00h35	5 18h00	5 22h15	7 08h35	7 18h20	7 21h10	8 12h35	7 15h35	7 08h20	5 19h30
1973	4 07h30	6 01h30	5 06h25	5 23h50	6 04h05	7 14h20	8 00h10	8 02h55	8 18h25	7 21h25	7 14h10	6 01h20
1974	4 13h20	6 17h15	5 12h15	6 05h40	6 09h55	7 20h10	8 05h55	8 08h45	9 00h15	8 03h15	7 20h00	6 07h10
1975	4 19h10	6 13h05	5 18h00	6 11h30	6 15h40	8 02h00	8 11h45	8 14h35	9 06h00	8 09h05	8 01h45	6 13h00
1976	5 00h55	5 18h55	4 23h50	5 17h15	5 21h30	7 07h50	7 17h35	7 20h25	8 11h50	7 14h50	7 07h35	5 18h45
1977	4 06h45	6 00h45	5 05h40	5 23h05	6 03h20	7 13h40	7 23h25	8 02h10	8 17h40	7 20h40	7 15h25	6 00h35
1978	4 12h35	6 06h30	5 11h30	6 04h55	6 09h10	7 19h25	8 05h10	8 08h00	8 23h30	8 02h30	7 19h15	6 06h25
1979	4 18h25	6 12h20	5 17h15	6 10h45	6 14h55	8 21h15	8 11h00	8 13h50	9 05h15	8 08h20	8 01h00	6 12h15
1980	5 00h10	5 18h10	4 23h05	5 16h30	5 20h45	7 07h05	7 16h50	7 19h40	8 11h05	7 14h05	7 06h50	5 18h00
1981	4 06h00	6 00h00	5 04h55	5 22h20	6 02h35	7 12h55	7 22h40	8 01h25	8 16h55	7 19h55	7 12h40	5 23h50
1982	4 11h50	6 05h45	5 10h45	6 04h10	6 08h25	7 18h40	8 04h25	8 07h15	8 22h45	8 01h45	7 18h30	6 05h40
1983	4 17h40	6 11h35	5 16h30	6 10h00	6 14h10	8 00h30	8 10h15	8 13h05	9 04h30	8 07h35	8 00h15	6 11h30
1984	4 23h25	5 17h25	4 22h20	5 15h45	5 20h00	7 06h20	7 16h05	7 18h55	8 10h20	7 13h20	7 06h05	5 17h15
1985	4 05h15	5 23h15	5 04h10	5 21h35	6 01h50	7 12h10	7 21h55	8 00h40	8 16h10	7 19h10	7 11h55	5 23h05
1986	4 11h05	6 05h00	5 10h00	6 03h25	6 07h40	7 17h55	8 03h40	8 06h30	8 22h00	8 01h00	7 17h45	6 04h55
1987	4 16h55	6 10h50	5 15h45	6 09h15	6 13h25	7 23h45	8 09h30	8 12h20	9 03h45	8 06h50	7 23h30	6 10h45
1988	4 22h40	5 16h40	4 21h35	5 15h00	5 19h15	7 05h35	7 15h20	7 18h10	8 09h35	7 12h35	7 05h20	5 16h30
1989	4 04h30	5 22h30	5 03h25	5 20h50	6 01h05	7 11h25	7 21h10	7 23h55	8 15h25	7 18h25	7 11h10	5 22h20
1990	4 10h20	6 04h15	5 09h15	6 02h40	6 06h55	7 17h10	8 02h55	8 05h45	8 21h15	8 00h15	7 17h00	6 04h10
1991	4 16h10	6 10h05	5 15h00	6 08h30	6 12h40	7 23h00	8 08h45	8 11h35	9 03h00	8 06h05	7 22h45	6 10h00
1992	4 21h55	5 15h55	4 20h50	5 14h15	5 18h30	7 04h50	7 14h35	7 17h25	8 08h50	7 11h50	7 04h35	5 15h45
1993	4 03h45	5 21h45	5 02h40	5 20h05	6 00h20	7 10h40	7 20h25	7 23h10	8 14h40	7 17h40	7 10h25	5 21h35
1994	4 09h35	6 03h30	5 08h30	6 01h55	6 06h10	7 16h25	8 02h10	8 05h00	8 20h30	8 23h30	7 16h15	6 03h25
1995	4 15h25	6 09h20	5 14h15	6 07h45	6 11h55	7 22h15	8 08h00	8 10h50	9 02h15	8 05h20	7 22h00	6 09h15
1996	4 21h10	5 15h10	4 20h05	5 13h30	5 17h45	7 04h05	7 13h50	7 16h40	8 08h05	7 11h05	7 03h50	5 15h00
1997	4 03h00	5 21h00	5 01h55	5 19h20	5 23h35	7 09h55	7 19h40	7 22h25	8 13h55	7 16h55	7 09h40	5 20h50
1998	4 08h50	6 02h50	5 07h45	6 01h10	6 05h25	7 15h40	8 01h25	8 04h15	8 19h45	8 22h45	7 15h30	6 02h40
1999	4 14h40	6 08h35	5 13h30	6 07h00	6 11h10	7 21h30	8 07h15	8 10h05	9 01h30	8 04h35	7 21h15	6 08h30
公元	春 SPRING			夏 SUMMER			秋 AUTUMN			冬 WINTER		

3 How to calculate the binomial of the day of birth

For practical purposes we shall use the Western calendar and take the same example, 19 August 1912, which we have already used. It is necessary first to find the serial number in the year of 19 August. Look at the first of the two following tables where the months are shown. Under August you will see that the 16th is the 228th day of the year. For the 19th add three days which gives us 231. Since 1912 was a leap year, add one more giving 232. It is also necessary to add a certain number for every year: look at the second table where you will see that the year 1912 has against it the figure 12. Add 12 to 232, the number we already have, which gives us 244 and then divide by 60 which leaves a remainder of 4. Four is thus the binomial we are looking for.

January		February		March		April		May		June	
1	16	1	16	1	16	1	16	1	16	1	16
1	16	32	47	60	75	91	106	121	136	152	167

July		August		September		October		November		December	
1	16	1	16	1	16	1	16	1	16	1	16
182	197	213	228	244	259	274	289	305	320	335	350

N.B. In a leap year, don't forget to add 1 to every date starting from 1 March.

1900	10	1920	54	1940	39	1960	24	1980	9
1901	15	1921	60	1941	45	1961	30	1981	15
1902	20	1922	5	1942	50	1962	35	1982	20
1903	25	1923	10	1943	55	1963	40	1983	25
1904	30	1924	15	1944	60	1964	45	1984	30
1905	36	1925	21	1945	6	1965	51	1985	36
1906	41	1926	26	1946	11	1966	56	1986	41
1907	46	1927	31	1947	16	1967	1	1987	46
1908	51	1928	36	1948	21	1968	6	1988	51
1909	57	1929	42	1949	27	1969	12	1989	57
1910	2	1930	47	1950	32	1970	17	1990	2
1911	7	1931	52	1951	37	1971	22	1991	7
1912	12	1932	57	1952	42	1972	27	1992	12
1913	18	1933	3	1953	48	1973	33	1993	18
1914	23	1934	8	1954	53	1974	38	1994	23
1915	28	1935	13	1955	58	1975	43	1995	28
1916	33	1936	18	1956	3	1976	48	1996	33
1917	39	1937	24	1957	9	1977	54	1997	39
1918	44	1938	29	1958	14	1978	59	1998	44
1919	49	1939	34	1959	19	1979	4	1999	49

4 How to calculate the binomial of the hour of birth

The usual practice of Chinese astrologers is to calculate the hour of birth according to Peking time. It is therefore necessary to make an adjustment depending in what part of the world you were born. For people born in Great Britain, for example, it is necessary to add eight hours to GMT.

The Chinese day is traditionally divided into twelve periods of two hours each. The first period begins at 2300 hours and lasts until 0100 hours the following day. (Each day begins at midnight.)

Thus the first period is from	2300 to 0100	seventh	1100 to 1300
second	0100 to 0300	eighth	1300 to 1500
third	0300 to 0500	ninth	1500 to 1700
fourth	0500 to 0700	tenth	1700 to 1900
fifth	0700 to 0900	eleventh	1900 to 2100
sixth	0900 to 1100	twelfth	2100 to 2300

The peak of each period is the hour in the middle.

N.B. The two-hour periods are *Yin* or *Yang* depending on whether they are even numbered or odd. The first period is *Yang* and the second *Yin* and so on.

The cycle repeats every five days. In order to find the number of the binomial for each period of a given day, it suffices to recall the figure which ends the serial number of the binomial of the day. If the figure is:

1 or 6 the series of periods starts in the	1st binomial
2 or 7	13th
3 or 8	25th
4 or 9	37th
5 or 0	49th

Thus in our given example, the person was born at 0700 GMT or 1500 hours Peking time, the beginning of the ninth period of the day. Since the binomial of the day of birth was 4, the first period of the day is the 37th binomial. The binomial number of the ninth period is therefore 45 (i.e.37 + 8).

N.B. If, when adjusting to Peking time, the hour of birth exceeds 24, then clearly the date changes to the next day.

Chapter 11

The Interpretation of the Four Binomials (Eight Signs)

The binomial has an importance of its own, but each of the two signs of which it is composed must also be studied separately. The two tables below show the reader how to find the ideograms (or signs) composing the binomials which we have discussed in the preceding chapter.

CLASSIFICATION OF THE SIXTY BINOMIALS

As you can see, each square contains two ideograms: the one on the left comes from the denary cycle and is repeated six times; the one on the right belongs to the duodenary cycle and is repeated five times.

1 This table classifies the binomials according to the denary signs which are the first elements in the binomials:

1	2	3	4	5	6	7	8	9	10
1 甲子	2 乙丑	3 丙寅	4 丁卯	5 戊辰	6 己巳	7 庚午	8 辛未	9 壬申	10 癸酉
11 甲戌	12 乙亥	13 丙子	14 丁丑	15 戊寅	16 己卯	17 庚辰	18 辛巳	19 壬午	20 癸未
21 甲申	22 乙酉	23 丙戌	24 丁亥	25 戊子	26 己丑	27 庚寅	28 辛卯	29 壬辰	30 癸巳
31 甲午	32 乙未	33 丙申	34 丁酉	35 戊戌	36 己亥	37 庚子	38 辛丑	39 壬寅	40 癸卯
41 甲辰	42 乙巳	43 丙午	44 丁未	45 戊申	46 己酉	47 庚戌	48 辛亥	49 壬子	50 癸丑
51 甲寅	52 乙卯	53 丙辰	54 丁巳	55 戊午	56 己未	57 庚申	58 辛酉	59 壬戌	60 癸亥

2 This table classifies the binomials according to the duodenary signs which are the second elements in the binomials:

I	II	III	IV	V	VI	VII	VIII	IX	X	XI	XII
1 甲子	2 乙丑	3 丙寅	4 丁卯	5 戊辰	6 己巳	7 庚午	8 辛未	9 壬申	10 癸酉	11 甲戌	12 乙亥
13 丙子	14 丁丑	15 戊寅	16 己卯	17 庚辰	18 辛巳	19 壬午	20 癸未	21 甲申	22 乙酉	23 丙戌	24 丁亥
25 戊子	26 己丑	27 庚寅	28 辛卯	29 壬辰	30 癸巳	31 甲午	32 乙未	33 丙申	34 丁酉	35 戊戌	36 己亥
37 庚子	38 辛丑	39 壬寅	40 癸卯	41 甲辰	42 乙巳	43 丙午	44 丁未	45 戊申	46 己酉	47 庚戌	48 辛亥
49 壬子	50 癸丑	51 甲寅	52 乙卯	53 丙辰	54 丁巳	55 戊午	56 己未	57 庚申	58 辛酉	59 壬戌	60 癸亥

When it comes to finding and defining your own signs, you can either use the ideograms themselves or their numbers.

Those readers who appreciate the almost magical quality which the signs have for the Chinese may prefer the ideograms. The chart overleaf shows the ideograms for the denary and duodenary cycles and how to write them. Their pronunciation in the Wade-Giles system is also shown, as well as the romanised form used in the Chinese People's Republic (in capital letters).

It may be simpler, however, for the reader to use letters or numbers. In the chart overleaf and throughout the rest of the book the denary ideograms are numbered 1 to 10 in Arabic numerals, and the duodenary I to XII in Roman numerals. When the binomial is given, the number of the ideogram from the denary cycle will be the digit of the binomial, remembering of course that all numbers ending in 0 represent 10. For ideograms from the duodenary cycle, divide all numbers over 12 by 12 and the remainder will be the number required.

To continue the example we have so far used:

Binomials		*The eight signs*		
Year	49	9	I	*Jen Tzŭ*
Month	45	5	IX	*Wu Shen*
Day	4	4	IV	*Ting Mao*
Hour	45	5	IX	*Wu Shen*

The twenty-two cyclic ideograms and how to write them.

甲	*Chia*	JIA	1	丑	*Ch'ou*	CHOU	II
乙	*Yi*	YI	2	寅	*Yin*	YIN	III
丙	*Ping*	BING	3	卯	*Mao*	MAO	IV
丁	*Ting*	DING	4	辰	*Ch'en*	CHEN	V
戊	*Wu*	WU	5	巳	*Ssŭ*	SI	VI
己	*Chi*	JI	6	午	*Wu*	WU	VII
庚	*Keng*	GENG	7	未	*Wei*	WEI	VIII
辛	*Hsin*	XIN	8	申	*Shen*	SHEN	IX
壬	*Jen*	REN	9	酉	*Yu*	YOU	X
癸	*Kuei*	GUI	10	戌	*Hsü*	XU	XI
子	*Tzŭ*	ZI	I	亥	*Hai*	HAI	XII

N.B. Draw the strokes in the order and in the direction indicated in the chart. Horizontal strokes (drawn from left to right) are drawn first and the vertical (from top to bottom) strokes next. Some of the strokes end in a hook turning inwards or outwards. Oblique strokes can be drawn upwards or downwards. The manner of writing is a rhythmic movement like a dance step, and this is why it is necessary to draw the strokes in order, even as a figure in a ballet.

When writing the signs it is important carefully to distinguish:

Chia and *Shen*: in the first the vertical stroke does not cross the square.
甲 申

Wu 戊 and *Hsü:* 戌		in the second character, there is an extra dot on the left hand downward stroke.
Chi 己 and *Ssŭ:* 巳		often confounded by the Chinese themselves, in the first the top part is left open.

N.B.

1. The two cycles, denary and duodenary, being even-numbered and starting simultaneously it follows that odd-numbered ideograms of the denary cycle must necessarily and exclusively be associated with the odd-numbered ideograms of the duodenary cycle. By the same token, even-numbered ideograms of each cycle are associated with each other.
2. Each odd-numbered ideogram of one cycle will thus be successively associated with the odd-numbered ideograms of the other cycle. The ideograms of the denary cycle will be repeated six times and those of the duodenary cycle five times giving thirty odd-numbered combinations. The same applies to even-numbered ideograms of each cycle which also make thirty even-numbered combinations.
3. Each odd-numbered binomial, like the two ideograms which it contains, has the qualities of *Yang*, that is to say: masculine, active, luminous, expanding, extroverted and positive in an electrical sense. Contrariwise each even-numbered binomial, together with its component characters, has the qualities of *Yin*, that is to say: feminine, passive, dark, receptive, introverted and negative.
4. Each binomial, as a unit, is linked with one of the Five Agents (Wood, Fire, Earth, Metal, Water) active in the Universe. This Agent differs from the Agents associated with the individual ideograms composing the binomial, and so three Agents are linked with each binomial, one with the binomial as a whole, two with each component separately.
5. Two successive binomials (alternately odd and even) are linked to the same Agent which becomes *Yang* and *Yin*, changing so to speak from positive to negative. For example, the binomials numbered 1 and 2 are linked to Metal, 3 and 4 to Earth, etc.

HOW TO INTERPRET BINOMIALS AND IDEOGRAMS (SIGNS)

At this stage the reader will know what his binomials and ideograms (signs) are and it is time to discuss their interpretation.

The denary and duodenary ideograms do not seem to carry much divinatory weight individually. In their relationships with each other, however, they are highly significant through the harmonies or oppositions which they reveal. Moreover, when they are concerned with defining the temperament of an individual or the possibilities of understanding between two people, they can be very revealing.

At this point it is worth emphasising that no element in a Chinese astrological theme should be considered in isolation or as something static. Its true weight is only revealed as a function of the whole.

The study of individual ideograms (signs) can show certain indications, but we must wait until all the data are assembled and compared before making a synthesis to produce a rounded picture.

Denary cycle

The following chart shows the affinities between the signs of the Denary cycle:

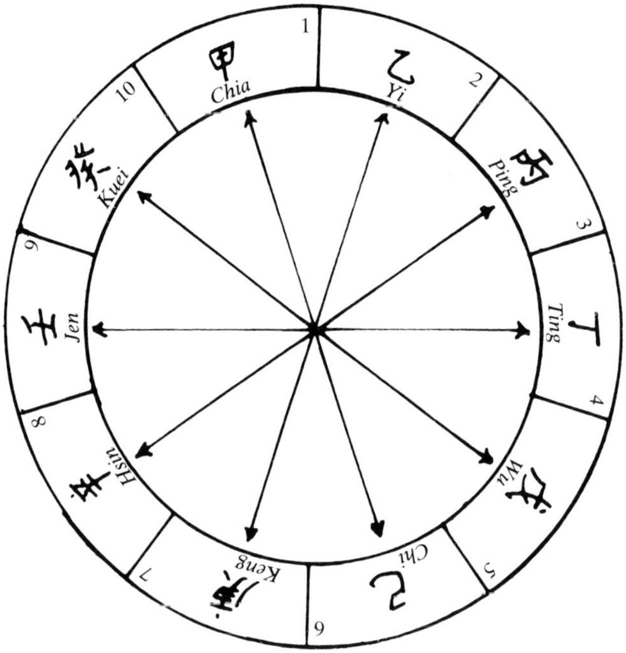
1
甲 Chia
2
乙 Yi
3
丙 Ping
4
丁 Ting
5
戊 Wu
6
己 Chi
7
庚 Keng
8
辛 Hsin
9
壬 Jen
10
癸 Kuei

Denary Cycle: Affinities

Opposite signs in the chart have a special affinity with each other. It is auspicious if such signs are found in two or more binomials in a person's horoscope. It is even more auspicious if one sign occurs in the binomial of the year and its opposite sign in the binomial of the hour. The relationship between signs 1 and 6 produces the Agent Earth, 2 and 7 the Agent Metal, 3 and 8 the Agent Water, 4 and 9 the Agent Wood, and between 5 and 10 the Agent Fire (see Chapters 12 and 13).

It is also auspicious if those

born in	Spring	have signs	1 or 2	in their binomials of the hour
	Summer		3 or 4	
	Dog Days		5 or 6	
	Autumn		7 or 8	
	Winter		9 or 10	

However, it is slightly unlucky if those born in Spring have either of the Autumn signs in their binomials of the hour; and if those born in Summer have the Winter signs in their binomials of the hour. The reverse is true in each case. In such cases the people concerned will have some difficulty in adapting themselves to life.

N.B. The dates of Chinese seasons are shown in the tables on pages 68 to 71. It should be noted that, for the Chinese, solstices and equinoxes are the apogee of each season and not the beginning. Thus in China the seasons begin 1½ months before seasons in the West.

Duodenary Cycle

The following charts show the affinities and oppositions existing between signs:

Tzŭ 子 I
Ch'ou 丑 II
Yin 寅 III
Mao 卯 IV
Ch'en 辰 V
Ssŭ 巳 VI
Wu 午 VII
Wei 未 VIII
Shen 申 IX
Yu 酉 X
Hsü 戌 XI
Hai 亥 XII

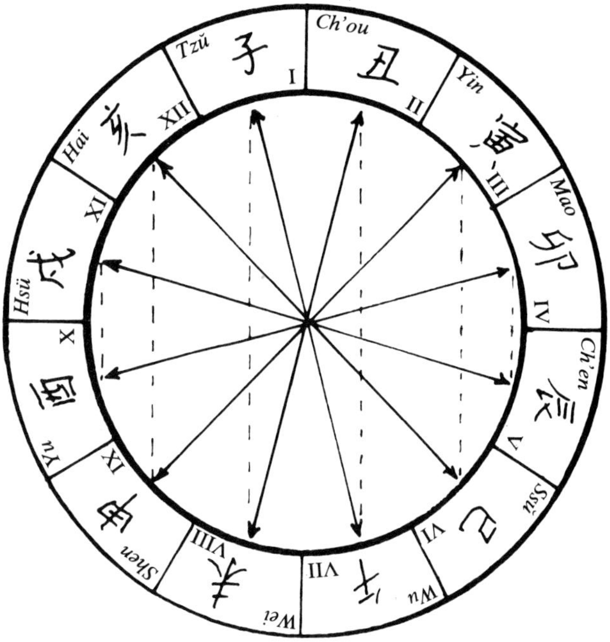

Tzŭ 子 I
Ch'ou 丑 II
Yin 寅 III
Mao 卯 IV
Ch'en 辰 V
Ssŭ 巳 VI
Wu 午 VII
Wei 未 VIII
Shen 申 IX
Yu 酉 X
Hsü 戌 XI
Hai 亥 XII

Affinities

Auspicious relationships – heavy lines *(Yang)*, light lines *(Yin)*

Sympathies – dotted lines

Oppositions

Inauspicious relationships – continuous lines

Antipathies – dotted lines

The relationships between the signs of the duodenary cycle are more revealing than those of the denary cycle.

In the left hand chart (affinities)

The signs connected by continuous lines have an auspicious relationship, and are therefore beneficial to each other. In Chinese astrology the triangle is especially auspicious. If the three signs of a triangle are found in three binomials of a horoscope, it indicates the greatest good fortune. These triangles are called respectively:

Water relationship	*Yang:*	I – V – IX
Metal relationship	*Yin:*	II – VI – X
Fire relationship	*Yang:*	III – VII – XI
Wood relationship	*Yin:*	IV – VIII – XII

The Earth relationship, which is indicated by the Square, is very auspicious too, and both *Yin* and *Yang*; it unites signs II, V, VIII, XI.

The signs connected by dotted lines have a sympathetic relationship between them.

In the right hand chart (oppositions)

The signs connected by continuous lines are inauspicious and even dangerous for each other. The signs connected by dotted lines are incompatible and antipathetic. If such signs appear in a person's horoscope it indicates a tendency to instability and inconsistencies of character.

Relationship between the signs of the Denary and Duodenary Cycles

The relationships between the signs of the duodenary cycle are more elaborate than those of the denary cycle. They are also more important in assessing the compatibilities and incompatibilities of different binomials.

The following table shows the special affinities between the signs of each cycle:

DUODENARY		&	DENARY		DUODENARY		&	DENARY		DUODENARY		&	DENARY	
I	子	&	9	壬	V	辰	&	5	戊	IX	申	&	7	庚
II	丑	&	6	己	VI	巳	&	4	丁	X	酉	&	8	辛
III	寅	&	1	甲	VII	午	&	3	丙	XI	戌	&	5	戊
IV	卯	&	2	乙	VIII	未	&	6	己	XII	亥	&	10	癸

Denary signs, as we saw in the chart on page 78, have no antipathies. When, however, a denary sign has an affinity with a duodenary one, it shares the antipathies of that sign. We see from the chart on page 79 that the duodenary sign 午 *wu* (VII) is opposed to the sign 子 *tzŭ* (I). Thus the binomials 丙子 *ping tzŭ* & 壬午 *jen wu* (3 I & 9 VII), are rather inauspicious as *Ping* (3) has an affinity for *Wu* (VII) and shares its antipathy for *Tzŭ* (I), & *Jen* (9) has an affinity for *Tzŭ* (I) and shares its antipathy for *Wu* (VII).

The relationships between the signs composing one binomial

Since this is only the first step in the study of a horoscope the Chinese do not consider it necessary to go into the relationship between binomial signs in too great detail. Below is a chart which gives what Chinese astrologers regard as sufficient to the purpose.

1	N	11	FS	21	W	31	FS	41	N	51	S
2	N	12	FS	22	W	32	FS	42	N	52	S
3	FS	13	W	23	FS	33	N	43	S	53	N
4	N	14	FS	24	W	34	N	44	N	54	S
5	S	15	FS	25	FS	35	S	45	FS	55	FS
6	FS	16	FS	26	S	36	FS	46	FS	56	S
7	N	17	FS	27	W	37	FS	47	N	57	S
8	N	18	FS	28	W	38	FS	48	N	58	S
9	FS	19	W	29	FS	39	N	49	S	59	FS
10	N	20	N	30	W	40	N	50	FS	60	S

N : Neutral S : Strong FS : Fairly strong W : Weak

The *Yin* and *Yang* aspects of Binomials and Signs

As odd numbers are *yang* (masculine) and even numbers are *yin* (feminine), it is better for a woman to be born in a *yin* year and for a man in a *yang* year. In the eight signs of a woman a predominance of *yin* is desirable; for a man a predominance of *yang*. However, the total absence of either *yin* or *yang* in a horoscope marks an incomplete and unstable character, for all excess is a fault. For example, it is almost as bad for a woman to have eight *yin* signs as it is to have eight *yang*.

CONCLUSION

We have noted that excess is a fault. It is possible to have an excess of harmony between the different signs of a horoscope. Such a character is so stable as to be lacking in vitality or energy.

Chapter 12

The Interaction of the Five Agents

The Five Agents are more commonly known as the five elements but I prefer the term Agents because they are not components of a substance.[43] Rather, for the Chinese, they symbolise five 'energies' which, sometimes *yin* and sometimes *yang*, act on nature. That is why none of these Agents should be considered in isolation, but in their relationships with all the others.

The Five Agents are the most important key to the interpretation of the horoscope. They may be positioned in a number of ways which define their mutual relationships and interdependence. Of these ways the two which serve our immediate purpose are: firstly, what is known as 'the order of Mutual Production' which conforms to the order of the seasons.

木 *mu*, WOOD engenders 火 *huo*, FIRE which engenders 土 *t'u*, EARTH (soil) which engenders 金 *chin*, METAL which engenders 水 *shui*, WATER which in its turn engenders WOOD and the cycle starts again.

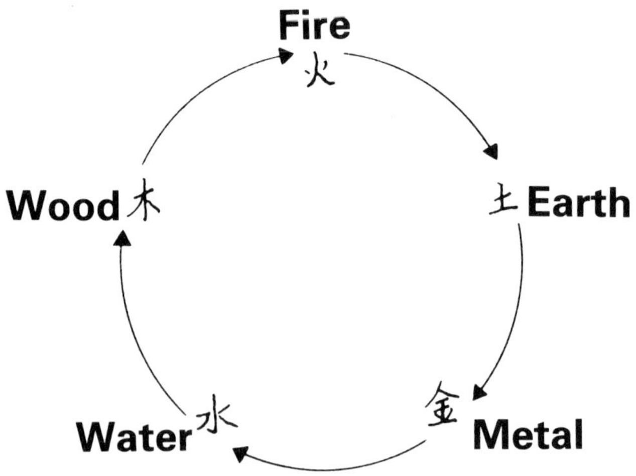
Fire
火
Wood 木
土 Earth
Water 水
金
Metal

The engendering Agent naturally protects and maintains the Agent which it produces. *This applies equally to anything which is in relationship with them, including the signs.*

The second way, which is derived from the first, is called 'the order of Mutual Conquest (or destruction)' Wood conquers Earth, Fire conquers Metal, Earth conquers Water, Metal conquers Wood, Water conquers Fire.

By combining these two orders, one can deduce two principles:

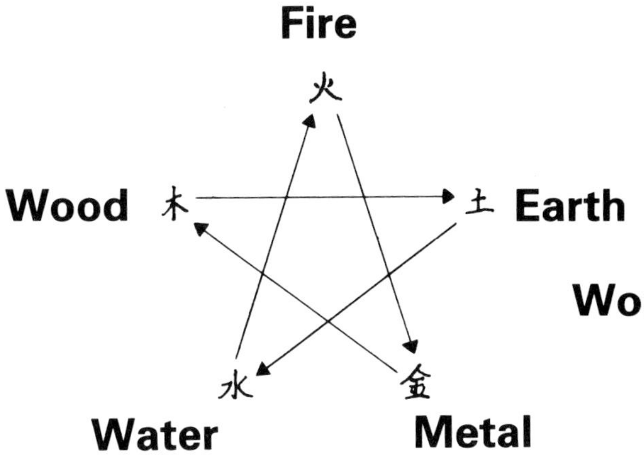

Fire
火
Wood 木
土 Earth
水
金
Water
Metal

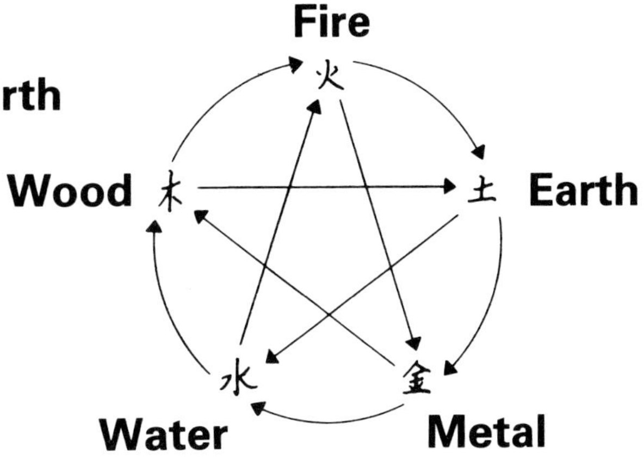

Fire
火
Wood 木
土 Earth
水
金
Water
Metal

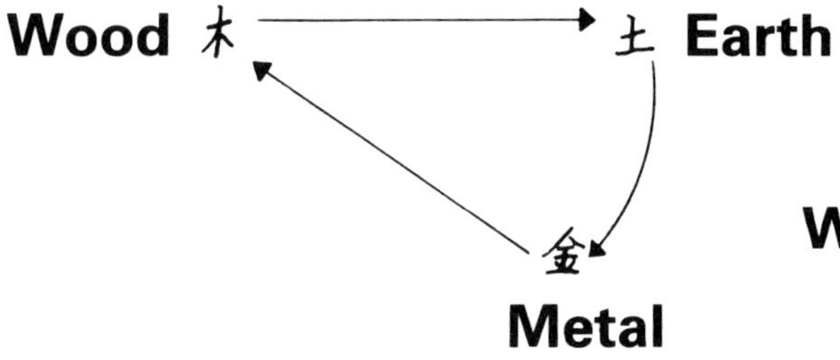

Wood 木
土 Earth
金
Metal

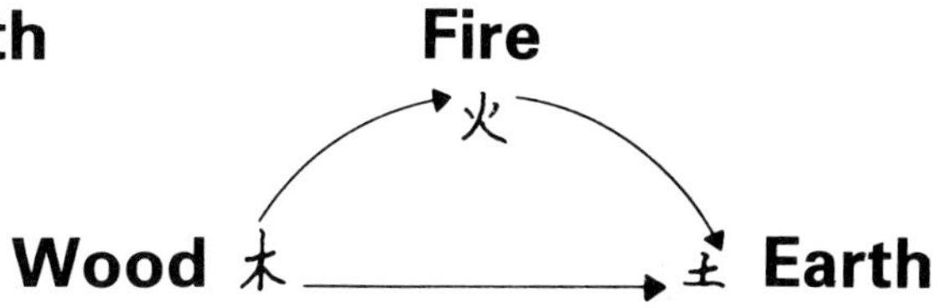

Fire
火
Wood 木
土 Earth

The principle of 'Control'

Wood conquers Earth, but Metal controls the operation for it comes to the help of Earth by attacking Wood. In the same way Fire conquers Metal but Water controls the operation. Earth conquers Water but Wood controls the operation. Metal conquers Wood but Fire controls the operation. Finally Water conquers Fire but Earth controls the operation.

The principle of 'Correction'

Wood conquers Earth, but Fire interrupts the process for it produces Earth and thus comes to its rescue; and as Wood produces Fire it can do nothing against it. Fire conquers Metal, but Earth interrupts the process. Earth conquers Water, but Metal interrupts the process. Metal conquers Wood, but Water interrupts the process. Water conquers Fire, but Wood interrupts the process.

These relationships are the most important element in establishing a horoscope. It is a good omen for all Agents to be present as it ensures equilibrium in a temperament. If one of the Agents is missing in a horoscope of a newly-born child, one tries to correct this by giving in its forename a character which contains the sign of the missing Agent.

RELATIONSHIP BETWEEN THE BINOMIALS AND THE AGENTS

To find the Agents which are associated with our binomials, we must now look at the following table, a full explanation of which is given below.

癸 壬	辛 庚	己 戊	丁 丙	乙 甲
酉 申	未 午	巳 辰	卯 寅	丑 子
金鋒劍	土傍路	木森大	火中爐	金中海
癸 壬	辛 庚	巳 戊	丁 丙	乙 甲
未 午	巳 辰	卯 寅	丑 子	亥 戌
木柳楊	金蠟白	土頭城	水下澗	火頭山
癸 壬	辛 庚	己 戊	丁 丙	乙 甲
巳 辰	卯 寅	丑 子	亥 戌	酉 申
水流長	木柏松	火靂霹	土上屋	水泉井
癸 壬	辛 庚	巳 戊	丁 丙	乙 甲
卯 寅	丑 子	亥 戌	酉 申	未 午
金泊金	土上壁	木地平	火下山	金中沙
癸 壬	辛 庚	巳 戊	丁 丙	乙 甲
丑 子	亥 戌	酉 申	未 午	巳 辰
木柘桑	金釧劍	土驛大	水河天	火燈覆
癸 壬	辛 庚	巳 戊	丁 丙	乙 甲
亥 戌	酉 申	未 午	巳 辰	卯 寅
水海大	木榴柘	火上天	土中沙	水溪大

◎六十甲子納音五行表

This Chinese table indicates the Agent related to each binomial in the sexagenary cycle. The table begins with the right hand column, each pair of signs (binomial) reading from top to bottom. Going from right to left two binomials are shown in each box and below each box is shown the Agent with which both binomials are associated. Each Agent is repeated six times, each time with a different poetical name; but the essential ideogram for the Agent is always included: 金 for Metal, 土 for Earth, etc. In the list which follows we give the binomials, the Agents with which they are associated and translations of the poetic names of the Agents.[44]

1	I	1	甲子	*chia tzŭ*	*Yang*	Metal	'gold at the bottom of the sea'.
2	II	2	乙丑	*yi ch'ou*	*Yin*		
3	III	3	丙寅	*ping yin*	*Yang*	Fire	'the fire of the furnace'.
4	IV	4	丁卯	*ting mao*	*Yin*		
5	V	5	戊辰	*wu ch'en*	*Yang*	Wood	'the tree of the great forest'.
6	VI	6	己巳	*chi ssŭ*	*Yin*		
7	VII	7	庚午	*keng wu*	*Yang*	Earth	'earth on the road side'.
8	VIII	8	辛未	*hsin wei*	*Yin*		
9	IX	9	壬申	*jen shen*	*Yang*	Metal	'steel of the sharp blade'.
10	X	10	癸酉	*kuei yu*	*Yin*		
1	XI	11	甲戌	*chia hsü*	*Yang*	Fire	'fire at the hilltop'.
2	XII	12	乙亥	*yi hai*	*Yin*		

3	I	13	丙子	*ping tzŭ*	*Yang*	Water	'water which enters and fertilises'.
4	II	14	丁丑	*ting ch'ou*	*Yin*		
5	III	15	戊寅	*wu yin*	*Yang*	Earth	'earth on the city wall' (defensive walls of the cities were often made of earth).
6	IV	16	己卯	*chi mao*	*Yin*		
7	V	17	庚辰	*keng ch'en*	*Yang*	Metal	'moulded bronze'.
8	VI	18	辛巳	*hsin ssŭ*	*Yin*		
9	VII	19	壬午	*jen wu*	*Yang*	Wood	'wood of poplar and willow'.
10	VIII	20	癸未	*kuei wei*	*Yin*		
1	IX	21	甲申	*chia shen*	*Yang*	Water	'water of rain and springs'.
2	X	22	乙酉	*yi yu*	*Yin*		
3	XI	23	丙戌	*ping hsü*	*Yang*	Earth	'earth of the roof'.
4	XII	24	丁亥	*ting hai*	*Yin*		
5	I	25	戊子	*wu tzŭ*	*Yang*	Fire	'fire of lightning'.
6	II	26	己丑	*chi ch'ou*	*Yin*		
7	III	27	庚寅	*keng yin*	*Yang*	Wood	'wood of cedar and pine' (symbols of longevity).
8	IV	28	辛卯	*hsin mao*	*Yin*		
9	V	29	壬辰	*jen ch'en*	*Yang*	Water	'running water'.
10	VI	30	癸巳	*kuei ssŭ*	*Yin*		
1	VII	31	甲午	*chia wu*	*Yang*	Metal	'gold in the mine'.
2	VIII	32	乙未	*yi wei*	*Yin*		
3	IX	33	丙申	*ping shen*	*Yang*	Fire	'fire at the foot of the hill'.
4	X	34	丁酉	*ting yu*	*Yin*		
5	XI	35	戊戌	*wu hsü*	*Yang*	Wood	'wood of the plain'.
6	XII	36	己亥	*chi hai*	*Yin*		
7	I	37	庚子	*keng tzŭ*	*Yang*	Earth	'earth of the wall'.
8	II	38	辛丑	*hsin ch'ou*	*Yin*		
9	III	39	壬寅	*jen yin*	*Yang*	Metal	'metal of the mirror'.
10	IV	40	癸卯	*kuei mao*	*Yin*		
1	V	41	甲辰	*chia ch'en*	*Yang*	Fire	'fire of the lamp'.
2	VI	42	乙巳	*yi ssŭ*	*Yin*		

3	VII	43	丙午	*ping wu*	*Yang*	Water	'water of the Celestial River' (the Milky Way is thus poetically called).
4	VIII	44	丁未	*ting wei*	*Yin*		
5	IX	45	戊申	*wu shen*	*Yang*	Earth	'earth of the great roads'.
6	X	46	己酉	*chi yu*	*Yin*		
7	XI	47	庚戌	*keng hsü*	*Yang*	Metal	'metal of bracelets and hairpins'.[45]
8	XII	48	辛亥	*hsin hai*	*Yin*		
9	I	49	壬子	*jen tzŭ*	*Yang*	Wood	'wood of mulberry'.
10	II	50	癸丑	*kuei ch'ou*	*Yin*		
1	III	51	甲寅	*chia yin*	*Yang*	Water	'water of streams'.
2	IV	52	乙卯	*yi mao*	*Yin*		
3	V	53	丙辰	*ping ch'en*	*Yang*	Earth	'earth buried in the sand'.
4	VI	54	丁巳	*ting ssŭ*	*Yin*		
5	VII	55	戊未	*wu wu*	*Yang*	Fire	'fire in heaven'.
6	VIII	56	己未	*chi wei*	*Yin*		
7	IX	57	庚申	*keng shen*	*Yang*	Wood	'wood of the pomegranate'.
8	X	58	辛酉	*hsin yu*	*Yin*		
9	XI	59	壬戌	*jen hsü*	*Yang*	Water	'water of the Ocean'.
10	XII	60	癸亥	*kuei hai*	*Yin*		

RELATIONSHIPS BETWEEN INDIVIDUAL SIGNS AND THE AGENTS

Each sign taken separately is associated with an Agent different from that linked to the binomial of which the sign is a part.

The Chinese recognise several relationships between signs and Agents, but here we take account only of those most commonly used in astrology.

Signs of the Denary Cycle

The denary signs, which form the first element of each binomial, are the oldest known cyclic signs. Originally they designated the days and, it seems, formed part of the names of persons born on the days when they appeared.[46]

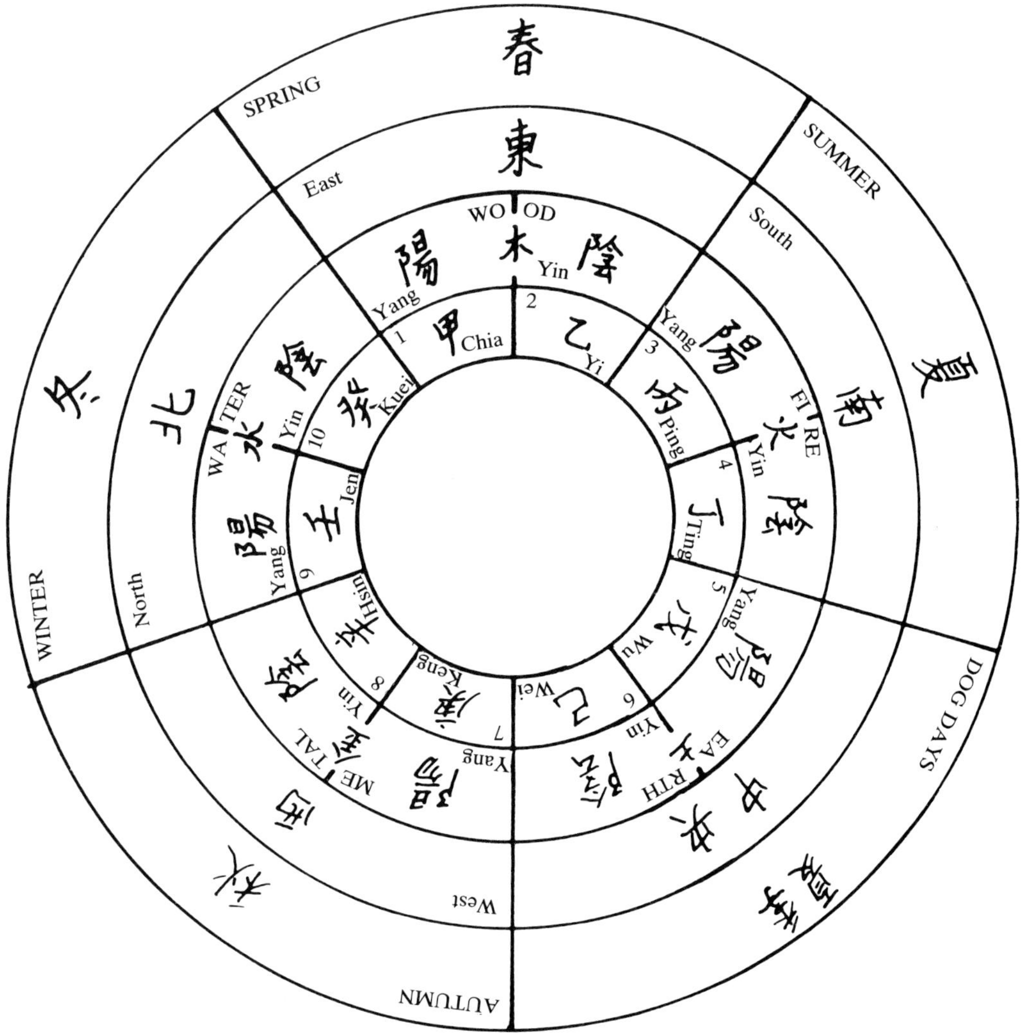
春
SPRING
SUMMER
東
East
South
WOOD
木
陽
陰
Yang
Yin
1
甲
Chia
2
乙
Yi
3
丙
Ping
4
丁
Ting
5
戊
Wu
6
Wei
7
庚
Keng
8
辛
Hsin
9
壬
Jen
10
癸
Kuei
FIRE
火
南
夏
WATER
水
北
North
WINTER
EARTH
土
中央
DOG DAYS
METAL
金
西
West
秋
AUTUMN

This chart indicates the affinities of the denary signs. Outside circle: the Seasons; second circle in: the points of the compass; third circle in: the Agents; left hand side *yang*; right hand side *yin*; innermost: the Denary Signs.

This chart shows the relationships between the denary signs, the Five Agents, the seasons and the points of the compass. As with binomials, each Agent is alternatively *yang* or *yin*, depending on which sign it is associated with.

In this, as in the following chart, in order not to have too many separate illustrations we show certain indications which will be explained in succeeding chapters.

Signs of the Duodenary Cycle

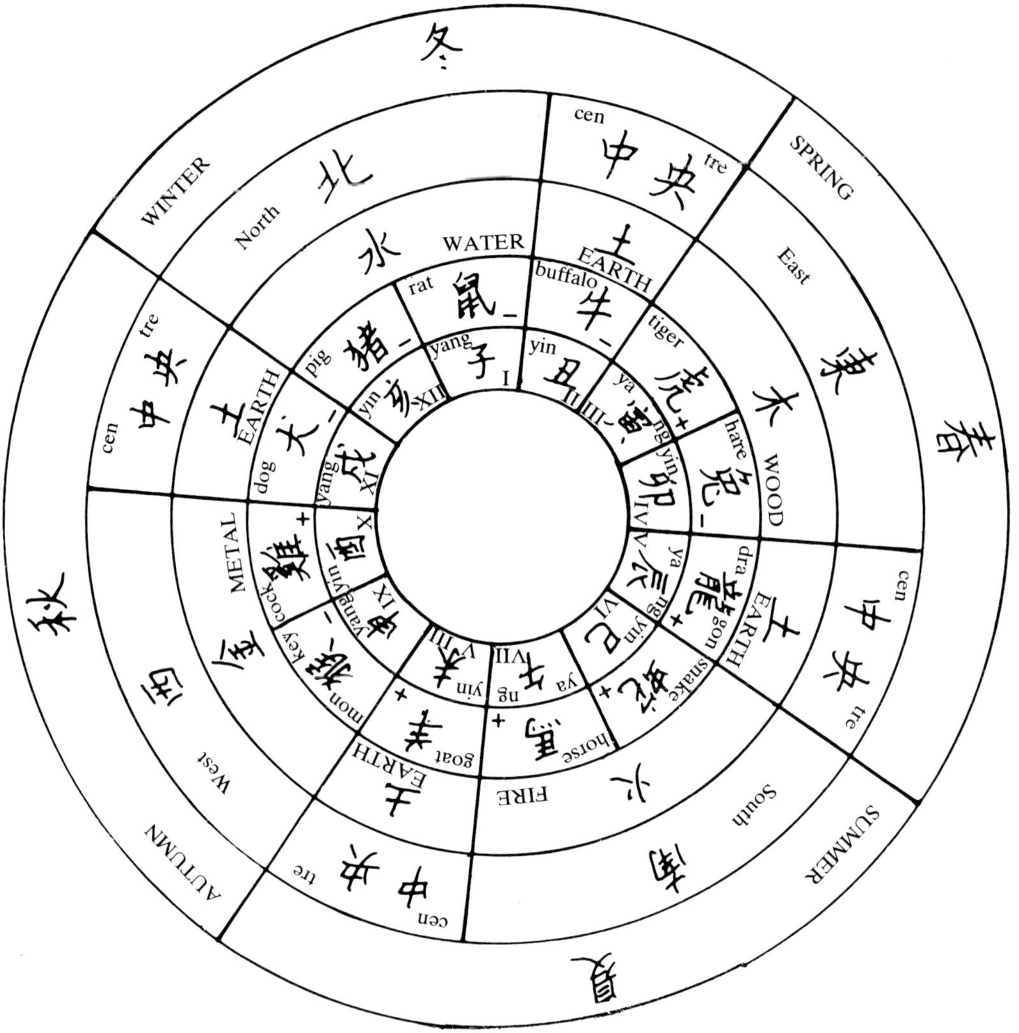
冬
WINTER
SPRING
春
SUMMER
夏
AUTUMN
秋
cen 中央 tre
North 北
East 東
South 南
West 西
WATER 水
EARTH 土
WOOD 木
FIRE 火
METAL 金
rat 鼠
buffalo 牛
tiger 虎
hare 兔
dragon 龍
snake 蛇
horse 馬
goat 羊
monkey 猴
cock 雞
dog 犬
pig 猪
yang 子 I
yin 丑 II
yang 寅 III
yin 卯 IV
yang 辰 V
yin 巳 VI
yang 午 VII
yin 未 VIII
yang 申 IX
yin 酉 X
yang 戌 XI
yin 亥 XII

5th (or outer) circle the four seasons.
4th circle the five points of the compass (centre being included).
3rd cycle the Five Agents.
2nd circle the twelve cyclical animals. A plus sign (+) in the lower right corner if they are *yang* and a minus sign (−) if they are *yin*. It will be noticed that the *yin* and *yang* quality of the animals does not necessarily follow that of the year.
1st (or inner) circle the duodenary cycle.
N.B. Since the Five Agents are the key factors of a personality, it is important to have each of them represented in a horoscope. According to their position in the horoscope their individual importance will vary.

For the Year The Agent associated with the binomial is the principal factor, being the key to the destiny of the person concerned.

The Agent associated with the duodenary sign is second in importance, being often associated in this case with an animal.

For the Month The Agent associated with the duodenary sign is the principal factor.

For the Day The Agent associated with the binomial represents good fortune, but the most important factor is the one associated with the denary sign.

For the Hour The Agent associated with the duodenary sign, and often associated with an animal, is the most important. It gives the most intimate indications of the inner self; for this reason many astrologers attach more importance to the hour than to the year whose indications are considered to be too vague and general. Indeed when Chinese astrologers establish what is known as a short horoscope only four signs are used: the duodenary sign of the month, the denary sign of the day and the two signs of the hour. Thus it will be seen that the year of birth often carries less weight than the hour, day or even month.

Chapter 13

Interpretation of the Five Agents

The Five Agents are forces in nature which act sometimes together and sometimes against each other. Their type of action is illustrated by their order of production.

Water produces Wood, but destroys Earth, etc. It represents the life-giving principle but is also associated with cold and severity. Wood gives form to life and represents creative imagination, to which Fire brings fruition, since, for the Chinese, Fire gives birth to humidity and luxuriant vegetation. It represents passion though not necessarily the passion of love. Earth represents the return to the Centre, which is equilibrium and provides the necessary realism without which nothing can exist. Metal provides the means for man's action on things and living creatures and therefore represents determination and will power.

Naturally the aspect of an Agent varies according to whether it is *yin* or *yang*. For example, Metal (will power), if *yang*, is an expanding active force, if *yin*, a concentrating force more like obstinacy than will power.

Here now are more detailed interpretations of the Five Agents. They are essentially drawn from the *Nei Ching* and completed by oral tradition.[47]

INTERPRETATION OF THE WOOD AGENT

In the Heavens the East engenders the wind, which on Earth engenders Wood.

Wood is linked to the morning and to spring. In the human body the organ which corresponds to it is the liver, the savour of which is acid. Its nature is temperate, its virtue Harmony, its qualities beauty and elegance. It promotes and leads. Its passion is anger. It runs the danger of downfall and perdition and by excess becomes its opposite. Quick tempered and susceptible, its bearing nevertheless always remains dignified. In a State, Wood corresponds to the Minister of Agriculture and to a relaxed style of government.

It represents creative power: artistic creativity, imagination, poetry, liberty. It can produce artists, poets or farmers.

Physical Type[48] The Wood individual is usually tall and thin and very straight. Complexion olive, fine eyes, full beard, red lips, hands and feet fine and small, soft skin. It would be inauspicious if his complexion was too clear for this would indicate the influence of Metal which is harmful to Wood. Contrariwise a dark complexion would be a good augury because this would come from Water which engenders Wood. However, if he is too weakly a certain amount of Metal can only be salutary.

INTERPRETATION OF THE FIRE AGENT

In the Heavens the South engenders the heat, which on Earth engenders Fire.

Fire is linked to midday, to the middle of summer. Organ: heart. Savour: bitter. Its nature is hot. Its virtue is brilliance (almost ostentation). Its quality prosperity, it burns and changes rapidly. Its danger is in its destructive power. Its emotional state is joy. In the State it corresponds to the Minister of War, its style of government is both enlightened and brilliant.

Violent and irascible, it represents passion, high spirits and ardour, but also lucidity for it is gifted with foresight. A temperament suitable for soldiers and men of action.

Physical Type Complexion high coloured, often ruddy. The face should be larger at the bottom. Nose aquiline, ears with detached lobes. Hair and beard verging on chestnut. It would be inauspicious to be fat or to have too large eyes, mouth and ears: these are the characteristics of the Water type and Water extinguishes Fire. The characteristics of Wood – straight and slim figure – would be auspicious for him.

INTERPRETATION OF THE EARTH AGENT

In the Heavens the Zenith engenders humidity, which on Earth engenders Earth.

Earth is linked to the beginning of the afternoon, and to the Dog Days (the humid period of Summer in North China). Organ: spleen; savour: sweet. Its virtue by reason of its humidity is to impregnate and to penetrate, with the danger of rotting, flooding and total submersion. Its quality is abundance, its action slow transformation. Endowed with thought and meditation. In the State it corresponds to the Minister of Home Affairs, and to a style of government based on prudence.

It corresponds to realism, to love of work, to hard working fecundity, to prudence. Temperament suitable to a businessman, financier.

Physical Type Yellow complexion; heavy, thick and solid features, such as the ears, eyes, nose and mouth. Full eyebrows, round back, flat belly (like the tortoise symbol of the earth). It would be inauspicious for him to have a beard and thick and bushy hair or to be thin with protruding bones: these would be the characteristics of the Wood type, Wood being inimical to Earth. Contrariwise a ruddy complexion is auspicious for it is a characteristic of Fire which engenders Earth.

INTERPRETATION OF THE METAL AGENT

In the Heavens the West engenders aridity, which on Earth engenders Metal.

In China the West wind comes from the steppes, whereas the East wind comes from the sea and brings fertility.

Metal is linked to Autumn and to the evening. Organ: lung. Savour: acrid. Its nature is fresh. Its virtues are clarity and purity (chastity above all for women). Its qualities are firmness and a capacity to realise its aims; it marks the harvest. Its danger comes from its destructive character which leads to a cessation of activity. Dependable and constant, its passion is solicitude, which can transform itself into moroseness and spiritual affliction. Endowed with eloquence, in the State it corresponds to the Minister of Justice and to an energetic type of government.

In short it symbolises will, rigidity, integrity. It is a temperament suitable for a man of the law, a jurist, a barrister.

Physical Type Clear complexion, straight ears, good general appearance. Square face, even lips and teeth. Extremity of the fingers small and square. It would be inauspicious to have a pointed head and nose and a complexion habitually ruddy, for they are characteristic of Fire, but is very auspicious to be robust for the Earth gives birth to Metal. If there is an excess of coldness a touch of Fire would be a good influence.

INTERPRETATION OF THE WATER AGENT

In the Heavens the North engenders cold, which on Earth engenders Water.

Water in Chinese astrology is not primarily thought of as a source of fertility but rather under its aspect of coldness and ice. Water is linked to Winter and to the night. Organ: kidney. Savour: salty. Its nature is very cold. Its virtues severity, rigidity, absence of passion. Its behaviour engenders respectful fear. Water invigorates but can be deadly. It is fearful and a bit timorous. It has the ability to listen. In the State it corresponds to the Ministry of Labour and a calm type of government.

Water has prolific power but is too self restrained, too calm and shut in upon itself. This temperament is suitable for tradespeople and artisans.

Physical Type Characterised by roundness: podgy, large and fat ears and thick lips, soft and supple skin, glossy hair, plump hands. It would be particularly inauspicious to have lobeless ears and lustreless eyes, or a runny nose and an habitually half open mouth, for those are signs of Earth influence. Contrariwise, it would be auspicious to have a clear complexion which would denote the action of Metal. Corpulence and soft flesh endanger the chance of having descendants.

All that we have discussed in this chapter shows how closely the Chinese see the Five Agents as associated with nature. It must be remembered, however, that they are symbols of forces acting in nature. They must not be confused with the material elements such as water, fire, etc., we use in everyday life.

STUDY OF RELATIONSHIPS BETWEEN THE FIVE AGENTS, THE CYCLIC SIGNS AND THE BINOMIALS

The relationships between the three Agents of each of the sixty binomials will now be analysed. This will help us to understand more clearly the real value of each binomial.

We must, of course, bear in mind what we have already said on the subject of the relative importance of each depending on whether it is associated with the binomial of the year, the month, the day and the hour, and accordingly make the necessary correction.

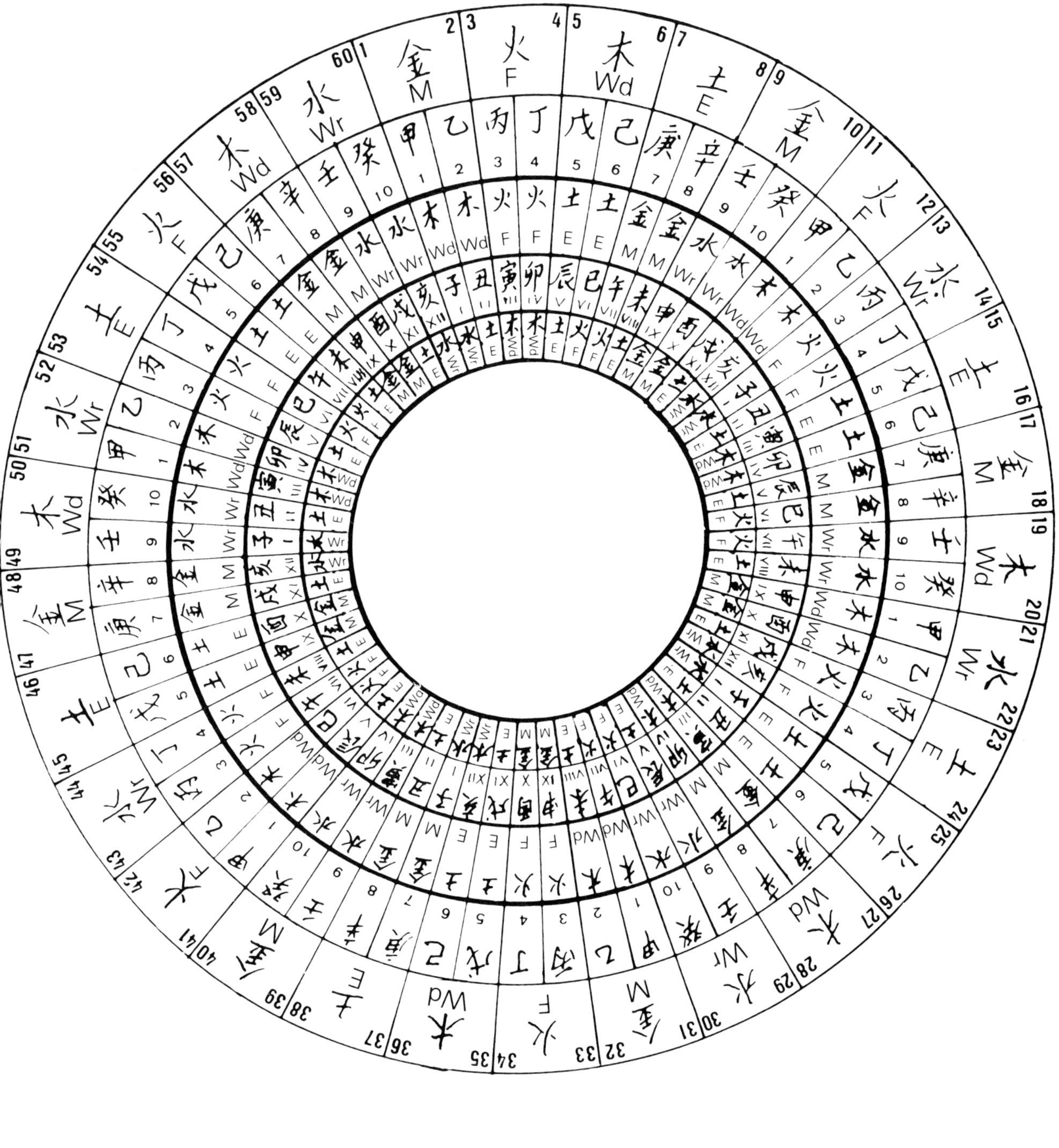

Wd = WOOD F = FIRE E = EARTH M = METAL Wr = WATER

The chart enables us to see at a glance the relationship between the Agents and the cyclic signs as arranged in five concentric circles. In the outer circle we find the numerical order of the binomials and the Agents associated with them. Each Agent, alternatively *Yin* and *Yang*, is associated with two successive binomials.[49]

In the next circle (the 2nd) we have the signs of the Denary Cycle and, in the circle below, the Agents with which they are associated. Then, in the next circle (the 4th), the signs of the Duodenary Cycle with, in the innermost circle, the Agents with which they are associated.

We must always remember that, whatever the indications in each binomial may be, they must never be considered in isolation, but always in their relationships with the three other binomials of our destiny (see the examples of interpretation of a horoscope given in Chapter 18).

Finally, remember that the denary sign is the most significant in the binomial of the day and that the duodenary sign is predominant in the binomials of the year, month and hour.

Don't forget that the action of the Agent of the binomial of the day together with that of the binomial of the year governs the element of chance.

Examples:

Binomial No 1

The Agent of the binomial is Metal.
The Agent of the denary sign is Wood.
The Agent of the duodenary sign is Water.

When the denary sign is the most important (for the day), Wood does not act on Water. The combination is neutral.

When the duodenary sign is dominant (year, month and hour), Water engenders Metal which dominates Wood.

Binomial No 5

The Agent of the binomial is Metal.
The Agent of the denary sign is Earth.
The Agent of the duodenary sign is Earth.

In both cases Earth is strong and has nothing to fear from the domination of Metal. Some people think that the combination is too strong but much depends on the other binomials of the horoscope.

Binomial No 15

The Agent of the binomial is Earth.
The Agent of the denary sign is Earth.
The Agent of the duodenary sign is Wood.

If the denary sign is the most important, Earth cannot act on Wood but is reinforced against the action of Wood.

If the duodenary sign is the most important, Earth dominates Wood as its action is reinforced by the Agent of the binomial.

Binomial No 26

The Agent of the binomial is Fire.
The Agent of the denary sign is Earth.
The Agent of the duodenary sign is Earth.

Earth is dominant and in all cases is reinforced by Fire.

Binomial No 54
The Agent of the binomial is Earth.
The Agent of the denary sign is Fire.
The Agent of the duodenary sign is Fire.

Two Fires make for strength and in all cases generate Earth and thus the relationship is auspicious.

Binomial No 60
The Agent is Water for the binomial and for the two signs.

The combination is excessive and therefore dangerous; but much depends on the other binomials of the horoscope.

Further examples of the relationships between the Agents can be found on pages 120 to 122 in the description of the relationships between man and wife. These can be applied to any other relationships between the Agents, man being considered as the dominating partner.

A very old Taoist document,[50] which instances favourable days for leaving the world and entering upon a solitary life suitable to contemplation, gives another very significant list based on the relationships existing between the Agents of the denary signs and those of the duodenary signs. According to this system, days are divided into five categories:

A	Precious days:	the Agent of the denary sign engenders that of the duodenary sign.
B	Convenient days:	the Agent of the duodenary sign engenders that of the denary sign.
C	Neutral days:	the two Agents are identical.
D	Days of opposition:	the Agent of the denary sign dominates that of the duodenary sign.
E	Days of struggle:	the Agent of the duodenary sign dominates that of the denary sign.

From this follows the table given below:

1	B	11	D	21	E	31	A	41	D	51	C
2	D	12	B	22	E	32	D	42	A	52	C
3	B	13	E	23.	A	33	D	43	C	53	A
4	B	14	A	24	E	34	D	44	A	54	C
5	C	15	E	25	D	35	C	45	A	55	B
6	B	16	E	26	C	36	D	46	A	56	C
7	E	17	B	27	D	37	A	47	B	57	C
8	B	18	E	28	D	38	B	48	A	58	C
9	B	19	D	29	E	39	A	49	C	59	E
10	B	20	E	30	D	40	A	50	E	60	C

CONCLUSION

The indications given by each Agent are sometimes contradictory. Nevertheless, the Agents are the surest means of defining the temperament of an individual. In Chapter 18 we give practical examples of this.

Chapter 14

The Twelve Animals

Each duodenary sign is also associated with an animal but the association is taken into account only for the year and by some for the hour.[51] For practical purposes they have the same number as their matching signs (see chart, page 79). They belong, however, to a separate, though parallel, cycle and must not be confused with the duodenary signs for they are not *yin* and *yang* in the same way:

yang	*Tzŭ*	is associated with the Rat *yin*
yin	*Ch'ou*	is associated with the Buffalo (Ox) *yin*
yang	*Yin*	is associated with the Tiger *yang*
yin	*Mao*	is associated with the Hare *yin*
yang	*Ch'en*	is associated with the Dragon *yang*
yin	*Ssŭ*	is associated with the Snake *yang*
yang	*Wu*	is associated with the Horse *yang*
yin	*Wei*	is associated with the Goat *yang*
yang	*Shen*	is associated with the Monkey *yin*
yin	*Yu*	is associated with the Cock *yang*
yang	*Hsü*	is associated with the Dog *yin*
yin	*Hai*	is associated with the Pig *yin*

With the twelve animals we arrive at the easiest and most picturesque method of making a horoscope. It is also the best known in France thanks to Vietnam where it is very popular and it has also been described at length in many books. I need not therefore expand on a subject which has been covered elsewhere. It is, moreover, only a part of a complete horoscope which cannot take the place of the more detailed method of the eight signs.

For the Chinese these are transcendental animals chosen for their auspicious character. We should not be led into a naturalism which Chinese tradition does not justify.

1912
1924
1936
1948
1960
1972
1984
1996

1

The **RAT** is born under the sign of *charm*, but his apparent calm hides an extreme aggressiveness. Uncommunicative he keeps his thoughts and feelings to himself. Lively spirit, intellectual, he has a strong critical sense. Scrupulously thorough he occupies himself with details at the risk of forgetting essentials. Often too self-seeking. He uses his charm and knows how to get the maximum profit out of his friends; he can exhaust their patience by abusing them and by not always being very nice to them. He is full of ideas but has little of the courage necessary to realise them. He has to work hard all his life. If he can overcome his laziness and pay more attention to others he may be able, when he has reached full maturity, to recognise opportunities which can appear very suddenly. Despite a tendency to greed, he is extravagant on his own account and cannot deprive himself of things he wants. In love he is capable of devoting himself body and soul to the one he loves, without being loved in return. Rat is a good adviser although his own life is not always crowned with success. He brings luck to his friends who can only benefit from his presence and his advice. He will have better luck in life if he is born at night and in the summer.

1913
1925
1937
1949
1961
1973
1985
1997

2

The **BUFFALO** is born under the double sign of *equilibrium* and *tenacity*. Very sincere, he has much patience but also obstinacy and pigheadednes. Fond of solitude, he is not very given to the social life. Few friends but they are very faithful to him. Little luck in love for he is too fussy and distrustful. Intelligent, his is an original spirit although sometimes a bit narrow-minded; extremely active and hard working. When he pulls himself together he can become a leader of men for he inspires confidence. Not talkative, his appearance is somewhat unprepossessing; he is in fact warm, solid and reliable. Not generous with his money. Very clever with his hands. Very independent, he would do well to leave home soon for he has few true ties with his family. Happy youth, at a mature age he may know anxieties and difficulties, perhaps in conjugal matters.

Respectful of convention, the Buffalo cannot bear failure and this makes him a bad sportsman. It is auspicious for him to be born in winter and the beginning of spring.

The woman Buffalo is a bit too responsive to flattery which could ruin her. She will probably wear the trousers in the home.

1914
1926
1938
1950
1962
1974
1986
1998

3

The **TIGER** is born under the sign of *courage* and with independence of character, for, although born to command, he hates to obey. With an appearance of broadmindedness and tolerance, he dislikes interference. Ill tempered. His unthinking courage leads him to take risks which he enjoys. He has a great care for his own reputation and likes to be well spoken of. Likes to put himself forward and risks making enemies; he should beware of this. He likes to play the 'grand seigneur' without paying too much attention to detail and thereby encouraging critics. But if he keeps his word he will recover the respect he deserves. His character is generous and he is capable of any sacrifice for others, above all in love, but he is seldom repaid.

At the beginning of his life, he may know unstable conditions, but opportunities may occur which, if he knows how to seize them, will help him to achieve renown. Luck will smile on him if he is born between the rising and the setting of the sun.

A woman Tiger is intelligent, virtuous and sincere. However, in Vietnam, from fear of being called tigresses, women seldom admit to being born under this sign.

1915
1927
1939
1951
1963
1975
1987
1999

4

The **HARE** is born under the sign of *virtue*, but also of prudence. He likes calm and discreet comfort, he detests change. Gentle, reserved and discreet, he is also a wheedler. Intelligent and very intuitive, he quickly recognises strength and weakness. He likes to sparkle to the point of sometimes seeming pedantic. Very good memory. He is a little lacking in decision and his hesitation can make him miss opportunities. Not always fair; touchy and suspicious, he is an egotist in spite of his good natured appearance. Worldly, he likes a good time and can spend more than is reasonable to entertain his friends. His taste for ostentation can lead to failure. In love he is not very faithful and he sometimes lacks family spirit. His taste for sexual pleasure can even wreck his career. Youth and maturity are easy periods for him without preoccupations or worries, but in old age he is in danger of becoming morose. He should start saving early for his old age. It is better for him to be born in Summer.

1916
1928
1940
1952
1964
1976
1988
2000

5

The **DRAGON** is born under the sign of *luck*. He can succeed in anything. Determined character, full of life, he is a fighter. He follows only his own judgement and is generally just. Seldom agrees with his elders. Rather full of himself, too blunt, he cannot smooth his rough edges and is in danger of not succeeding socially. He is, however, admired, but his distrust for the opinion of others can make him fail to fulfil his destiny. Highly intelligent, with all the talents, his advice should always be given consideration. By contrast, always in a hurry, though reflective by nature, he risks making mistakes from error of judgement. He lacks patience and tolerance. If he can check his impulses and improve his ways, he will achieve success. The Dragon is often loved to the point of adulation, but he himself is seldom in love.

In his youth his obstinacy can prejudice his success. Like all very lucky people, he runs the risk of luck turning against him. It is inauspicious for a Dragon to be born on a stormy day.

The woman under this sign is very sure of herself and hates solitude.

1917
1929
1941
1953
1965
1977
1989
2001

6

The **SNAKE** is born under the sign of *wisdom*. Very stable character, very intelligent, the Snake loves to organise things. Of very high, sometimes excessive, morality and a bit of a sanctimonious hypocrite. Likeable and respected, not very talkative, he is a very reflective, intelligent and intuitive thinker, but he is incapable of listening to the advice of others. Calm, determined and stubborn, he cannot bear failure and is a poor sportsman. In his heart of hearts he is sometimes wicked and jealous. Very sociable, he knows how to construct relationships but not always in a lasting way. He is easily upset and sometimes shows himself to be narrow minded. Very inclined to matters of love, he is exclusive and jealous, although the male Snake may not always be a model of fidelity. Lucky in money matters, in his love of discussion he risks losing opportunities. The Snake does not lack courage. He has very good taste and knows how to appreciate beautiful things.

His youth is often difficult; in maturity he will know the pangs of love. If he can prepare himself for old age, luck will smile on him. The hotter it is on his birthday, the happier he will be.

The woman Snake is an excellent housewife.

1918
1930
1942
1954
1966
1978
1990
2002

7

The **HORSE** is born under the double sign of *elegance* and *ardour*. Lively, speedy, quick tempered but kindly. Always impatient, he loves journeys, change, the world and the easy life. He always likes to be in the limelight. Very sociable, he makes friends easily and likes to be helpful. He takes little account of others' advice and is brilliant rather than truly intelligent. He has a genius for making the most of opportunities which can lead him to success. He is basically loyal. In love he is weak and in spite of his egotism he is capable of all sacrifices. A true rabble rouser, he is able to lead the crowd although he lacks judgement and lets himself be carried away by his own eloquence. He has the bad habit of talking too much and he cannot keep a secret. His constant opportunism is in danger of making enemies for himself. His taste for ostentation and his boastfulness are equally irritating. However, if he can control himself and bridle his passions, his ambition can lead him to success. It is very favourable for him to be born in Winter.

1919
1931
1943
1955
1967
1979
1991
2003

8

The **GOAT** is born under the sign of *art*. With his sweet and easy going character, he adapts easily to all circumstances, for he is by nature dependent. This is also why he is endowed with a great deal of filial spirit. Intuitive and full of subtlety, he has good taste and artistic feeling, and a love of Beauty. He tries hard to improve but sometimes lacks method; this taste for perfection may lead him to matters of religion and piety. Quite irresponsible (as an artist he will willingly accept patronage), he fears taking initiatives, although if necessary he can take charge with plenty of decision and economy: for he does not lack will when it is necessary to achieve his ends. He is good at avoiding disagreements. For the sake of a peaceful life he forgives easily; but he fails to recognise his own misdeeds and is capable of extremely bad faith. He is changeable and whimsical. His love affairs are troubled and superficial, and in marriage he is off-handed. In order to succeed he should cure himself of a tendency towards instability and eccentricity. It is good if it is raining at his birth.

1920
1932
1944
1956
1968
1980
1992
2004

9

The **MONKEY** is born under the sign of *fantasy*. All his behaviour is founded on a lively superiority complex. He likes jokes but seldom at his own expense. He likes bustle and movement and can create discord for his own amusement. Lively, active, agile he likes discussion, struggle and competition. Very selfish, he is, however, very diplomatic thanks to his inventive spirit. If he wants to, he can be extremely tactful. Likes to pass for a chivalrous person to get people to talk about him. He can lose time in busying himself with the affairs of others. He likes to strike attitudes and to play with words. He is not ashamed to lie. He has a certain tendency towards dishonesty which can lead him far astray if he does not take care. If he can cure himself of this he should go far for he is intelligent, cultivated and is thirsty for knowledge, qualities unhappily spoit by too much inconstancy. In love he is too unstable to find happiness. He is easily smitten but is too clear headed for lasting passion. All through his life there will be difficult periods, but he will always fall on his feet thanks mainly to his supreme capacity for clear thinking which is the basis of his character and his dominant quality. He would be well advised to be born in the summer.

1921
1933
1945
1957
1969
1981
1993
2005

10

The **COCK** is born under the sign of *candour*. He is fundamentally honest by nature. Very intelligent, he is perhaps a thinker. Vivacious with an excellent memory, he can be interesting even if he is a bit short of personality. Much above the ordinary, unhappily he likes to show off; he likes excursions, parties and is basically very vain. However, his brilliance guarantees him help from important people. Generous with a great gift for friendship, he can achieve success by strength of will, but he should master his unstable character which moves too easily from the heights to the depths. Very sure of himself, he is, however, preoccupied and anxious. If something is not to his liking, he worries too much about the slightest details thereby often forgetting essentials.

If the cock is born in spring, he will be less boastful.

The woman under this sign is very fond of eating, rather secretive and loves gossip. She lacks initiative.

1922
1934
1946
1958
1970
1982
1994
2006

11

The **DOG** is born under the sign of *loyalty* but also of anxiety. He attaches great importance to respect for the 'rites', has great honesty and moral sense. He also inspires confidence in his elders. An honest, active worker he can succeed in business and is the object of general esteem. He is a fighter, intelligent and clear in his judgements. Obstinate and active he also knows how to listen. His intuition warns him of danger, but, being rather pessimistic, he exaggerates it, whence his anxiety. This anxiety and his clear thinking mean that he is not very happy in love despite his warm nature. He is ambitious, extravagant and hot headed. If he cannot overcome his anxieties he has little chance of a happy life.

If he is born at night he will always be anxious.

Women under this sign are very seductive but they are changeable and they love luxury; they are rather narrow minded and without much patience. Their destiny cannot improve unless they correct their faults.

1923
1935
1947
1959
1971
1983
1995
2007

12

The **PIG** is born under the sign of *honesty*. Incapable of dissimulation, he always goes straight to the point. His heart is pure and without malice. He deserves confidence but can be easily swindled. Scrupulous, he likes to take the initiative by himself. He takes little thought for the future, and he is not one to go out drinking with friends. Besides, he can't hold his liquor. He is not made for social life. He does not care too much about his reputation. Outwardly calm and stable he is very wilful and obstinate. He likes money without seeming to. He loves discussion and is often a mischief maker. He is often mistaken and his arguments are weak. Credulous and suspicious, he is not far from being stupid. He often gives in without a struggle for he is tolerant and hates disputes.

It is not suitable for him to be born at the beginning of the year.

Women under this sign are lazy, suspicious and jealous and know how to fool people. In order to succeed they must correct their character and their narrow-mindedness.

These composite portraits, drawn in general terms, are traditional. They illustrate character types which do not exist in a pure state, for many other elements will modify them and complete them if you want to establish a true horoscope.

Chapter 15

The Twenty-Eight Constellations of the Zodiac Lunar Dwellings

The Chinese attribute a constellation to each day. In strict association with the agent of the binomial of the day, the constellation defines the share of good luck given to an individual throughout his life.[52]

Based, in theory at least, on the lunar dwellings in the course of one revolution, the constellations number twenty-eight. Since this number corresponds with four weeks and is exactly divisible by four, each constellation always returns on the same day of the week.

1897		1943	1965	1988	1
1898	1921	1944	1966		2
1899	1922		1967	1989	3
1900	1923	1945	1968	1990	4
1901	1924	1946		1991	5
1902		1947	1969	1992	6
1903	1925	1948	1970		7
1904	1926		1971	1993	8
	1927	1949	1972	1994	9
1905	1928	1950		1995	10
1906		1951	1973	1996	11
1907	1929	1952	1974		12
1908	1930		1975	1997	13
	1931	1953	1976	1998	14
1909	1932	1954		1999	15
1910		1955	1977	2000	16
1911	1933	1956	1978		17
1912	1934		1979	2001	18
	1935	1957	1980	2002	19
1913	1936	1958		2003	20
1914		1959	1981	2004	21
1915	1937	1960	1982		22
1916	1938		1983	2005	23
	1939	1961	1984	2006	24
1917	1940	1962		2007	25
1918		1963	1985	2008	26
1919	1941	1964	1986		27
1920	1942		1987	2009	28

The above table will help you to find the constellation of a birthday or any given day. Find first the serial number of the day (see page 72 above). Add to this number the number in the right hand column which corresponds with the year concerned. Divide the sum of the two numbers by 28 and the remainder, or 28, will be the number of the constellation. To continue with our example, 19 August 1912, we know that the serial number of the day is 232, the number corresponding with 1912 is 18. Add 232 to 18 which equals 250, divide by 28 and the remainder is 26 which is the number of the constellation concerned.

THE DAILY PREDICTIONS OF THE TWENTY-EIGHT CONSTELLATIONS

These predictions have from the first been used to define the auspicious and inauspicious character of a given day and they form the basis of more detailed horoscopes given in almanacs for each day of the year. These traditional horoscopes reflect the atmosphere of imperial China, when the official examinations were the only conceivable path to social promotion and when everything was subordinated to the welfare of the family group. Thus marriage and burials are very important and the manner in which any activity is begun, such as laying the foundations of a house, is vital in Chinese eyes. It is easy to apply these predictions to any occasion such as birth or a business appointment; all that is necessary is a little thought and concentration to extract their meaning. Then, if a prediction seems unfavourable, it is always possible to palliate what may be inconvenient in it by employing other divinatory elements. The Chinese make no bones about doing this.[53]

1 THE HORN, *Jupiter, Thursday* **auspicious**
'To whomsoever builds on this day, this constellation will bring glory and prosperity, and men of letters will be able to approach near to the throne of the Emperor. Marriages on this day will result in numerous posterity. But to repair a tomb or go to a funeral may provoke a new grief.'

2 THE NECK, *Venus, Friday* **inauspicious**
'Do not build on this day; let the eldest not take the succession; let nothing be undertaken for in the ten following days a disaster will occur. Funerals and marriages will cause untimely death and will risk leaving widows in the house.'

3 **THE ROOT,** *Saturn, Saturday* **inauspicious**

'To build on this day will be inauspicious enough, and the celĕbration of marriages will bring endless calamities. Journeys by boat will be shipwrecked. Funerals will cause the impoverishment of descendants.'

4 **THE CHAMBER,** *Sun, Sunday* **auspicious**

'To build today assures wealth and abundant prosperity. The Spirits of Happiness, of Longevity, of Honour, of Riches and of Glory hasten to meet you. If funerals are celebrated today, officials will be promoted three ranks.'

5 **THE HEART,** *Moon, Monday* **inauspicious**

'To build today will be most inauspicious and everything will lead to ruin sooner or later. Similarly burials and marriages will be seen to be disastrous and will assure three years of repeated calamities.'

6 **THE TAIL,** *Mars, Tuesday* **auspicious**

'To build today is to be assured of blessings and a numerous progeny. To undertake any business matter or to flood a paddy field will assure prosperity to descendants. Funerals and marriages will lead to the ennoblement of the family and the obtaining of posts in the Capital.'

箕水豹吉
馮異

7 **THE BASKET,** *Mercury, Wednesday* **auspicious**
'To build today gives an assurance of power, and the beginning of any enterprise will assure the family the greatest good fortune. Marriages and the repairing of tombs will be beneficent; coffers will overflow with gold and silver and the granaries with grain.'

斗木獬吉
朱祐

8 **THE LADLE,** *Jupiter, Thursday* **auspicious**
'To build today assures a supreme abundance of wealth. To put a tomb in order or to celebrate a funeral will assure descendants of prosperity. To open an establishment or to flood a paddy field will assure the multiplication of livestock. A marriage will be guaranteed happiness upon happiness.'

牛金牛凶
祭遵

9 **THE BUFFALO,** *Venus, Friday* **inauspicious**
'To build today will assure nothing but danger and calamities. Paddy fields and silkworms will bring no profit to the unhappy master. A marriage or the opening of a business will behold a sea of troubles, and livestock will suffer from it.'

女土蝠凶
景丹

10 **THE WOMAN,** *Saturn, Saturday* **inauspicious**
'To build today will be very damaging to the charm of pretty women and make brothers quarrel among themselves like wolves and tigers. Burials and marriages will cause luck to disappear and oblige the family to emigrate.'

11 THE VOID, *Sun, Sunday* **inauspicious**

'To build today will be calamitous. Boys and girls will sleep uncherished. A wind of debauchery will blow through the family from a lack of rites; and the wives of sons and grandsons will sleep in other beds.'

12 THE ROOF, *Moon, Monday* **inauspicious**

'Today nothing large should be built, and burial or the repairing of tombs will provoke effusions of blood. To open a business or to irrigate a paddy field will cause continual unhappiness and law suits.'

13 THE HOUSE, *Mars, Tuesday* **auspicious**

'To build today will bring an increase in land and livestock. Sons and grandsons will enjoy glorious careers. All enterprises will bring riches and prosperity in the dwelling. Marriages and funerals will take away care for ever.'

14 THE WALL, *Mercury, Wednesday* **auspicious**

'To build today will bring great prosperity; marriages will cause only peace and joy. Funerals will assure wealth and prosperous descendants. To start an enterprise or to irrigate a paddy field will assure progeny.'

15 THE LEGS, *Jupiter, Thursday* **inauspicious**

'To build today will be very auspicious, Harmony and Prosperity will blow through the door of the family home. But a burial today will produce a mysterious death, and to do business or to flood a paddy field will only attract calamities.'

16 THE TIE, *Venus, Friday* **auspicious**

'To build columns today is equivalent to building up to the gate of Heaven: the family will see its riches increase and everything will prosper. Today's marriages will be fruitful, and descendants will gain honours and social promotion.'

17 THE STOMACH, *Saturn, Saturday* **auspicious**

'To whomsoever builds this day everything comes like a wind blowing riches and precious glory, and innumerable joys will be his. Funerals will assure social promotion and marriages will see the flourishing of complete harmony.'

18 THE LIGHTS, *Sun, Sunday* **inauspicious**

'To build today would be like letting a buffalo into the paddy field. Funerals will bring incessant worry. To begin anything will surely lead to calamities, and marriages will only engender misery.'

畢月烏吉
陳俊

19 THE THREAD, *Moon, Monday* **auspicious**
'Light will shine on him who builds. Paddy growing and silkworm breeding will know years of abundance. Luck and blessings will flow to your door. Marriages and funerals will procure a doubled longevity.'

觜火猴凶
傅俊

20 THE TURTLE, *Mars, Tuesday* **inauspicious**
'To build today will invite a lawsuit. Celebrate a funeral and before long the house will collapse; at least three deaths will follow, and reserves of provisions will dwindle away.'

參水猿凶
杜茂

21 THE THREE ASSOCIATES, *Mercury, Wednesday* **auspicious**
'To build today will bring ample prosperity. The star of the lettered person will bring light. Irrigation of the paddy field and business will be under happy auspices. But funerals and marriages will shatter the family.'

井木犴吉
姚期

22 THE WELL, *Jupiter, Thursday* **auspicious**
'To build today will bring prosperity to paddy fields and silkworm breeding. The family name will be the first on the golden list. In the case of funerals, take extra care if the deceased has died a violent death. Every enterprise will bring money and numerous inheritors.'

23 THE SPIRIT, *Venus, Friday* **inauspicious**
'Under this inauspicious star, building will cause disappearances and the threshold will no longer have a master. The celebration of funerals will procure advancement but a marriage will see a woman lonely in the nuptial chamber.'

24 THE WILLOW, *Saturn, Saturday* **inauspicious**
'To build today will lead to trouble in the courts; and disasters and thieves will put the house in danger. Funerals and marriages will be the prelude to a series of miseries.'

25 THE STAR, *Sun, Sunday* **inauspicious**
'This day is good for building houses, and prosperity and advancement will lead to the feet of the Emperor. But to celebrate a funeral or to proceed with irrigation will cause the wife to abandon her hearth and look for another man.'

26 THE FISHING NET, *Moon, Monday* **auspicious**
'On this day if a pavilion is built all descendants who are officials will approach the Emperor. To celebrate funerals and to flood the paddy fields will attract money and riches. Marriages will be the cause of unending harmony and happiness.'

27 THE WINGS, *Mars, Tuesday* **inauspicious**

'Construction of a high building should be avoided, for this will cause the death of successive masters of the house. Marriages and funerals will not bring prosperity. Young girls will run after boys away from home.'

28 THE CHARIOT, *Mercury, Wednesday* **auspicious**

'To build under these auspices will attract promotion. A marriage will receive the Emperor's blessing. To celebrate funerals will make bright the star of the lettered person. Prosperity will equal a cairn of gold and a mountain of jade.'

Chapter 16

The Song of the Four Seasons

The Chinese insist on the importance of starting any action or enterprise at a favourable time. In their view such a time occurs at the apogee of the curve of any given period.

During a lunar month, the most auspicious influences will begin with the first quarter, culminate at full moon and thereafter decrease. The full moon, therefore, is always auspicious and particularly that of the 8th moon, the time of the moon festival.

Similarly, in a period of two hours the most influential time, and therefore the most favourable, is in the middle. In the West this means every even-numbered hour: midnight, 0200, 0400, midday, etc.; for Chinese two hourly periods begin with odd-numbered hours.

We have previously remarked that Chinese seasons culminate at solstices and equinoxes. Thus, in China,

Spring	begins about	5	February
Summer		5	May
the Dog days		22	July
Autumn		7	August
Winter		7	November

That part of the Chinese popular almanac which I show here is based on the more or less auspicious worth of the hour of birth which is defined, depending on the season, by the duodenary sign.[54]

As seen earlier in the book, the denary signs also may be more auspicious at certain times: 1 and 2 in Spring, 3 and 4 in Summer, 5 and 6 in the Dog Days, 7 and 8 in Autumn, 9 and 10 in Winter.

THE 'SONG OF THE FOUR SEASONS' HORARY PREDICTION

The following song which is found in all almanacs shows the share of luck given to you according to the hour of your birth, indicated by your duodenary sign. The signs of the twelve branches are placed on various parts of the body of four little figures (one per season) representing the Yellow Emperor, Huang ti.

According to the season the part of the body where the sign is changes. Bearing in mind, therefore, the season of your birth, without forgetting that in China the season begins and ends one and a half months earlier than in the West, all you have to do is to find that part of the body where your sign of the hour is.

Each season has a symbolic flower: the peony for spring, the lotus for summer, the chrysanthemum for autumn and the plum – opposite – for winter.

SPRING
(Begins 4/5 February)

季
春

Head		VII	
Shoulders	VI		VII
Belly	IV		XI
Hands	V		IX
Sex		I	
Knees	XII		X
Feet	III		II

N.B. I have given the locations of the twelve characters according to an ancient little book from which the pictures are taken. The more common locations found in modern almanacs are slightly different and I show them below for those who may prefer them.

季
春

Head		I	
Shoulders	IV		X
Belly	II		XII
Hands	VI		VIII
Sex		VII	
Knees	V		XI
Feet	IX		III

SUMMER
(Begins 5/6 May)

季
夏

Head		I	
Shoulders	II		VIII
Belly	IV		X
Hands	VI		XII
Sex		VII	
Knees	V		XI
Feet	IX		III

季
夏

Head		VII	
Shoulders	IV		X
Belly	VIII		XII
Hands	VI		II
Sex		I	
Knees	V		XI
Feet	III		IX

AUTUMN

(Begins 7/8 August)

季
秋

Head	III	
Shoulders	I	VII
Belly	VIII	II
Hands	IV	X
Sex	IX	
Knees	V	XI
Feet	XII	VI

秋

Head	XII	
Shoulders	I	VII
Belly	IV	VIII
Hands	VI	II
Sex	IX	
Knees	III	X
Feet	XI	V

WINTER
(Begins 7/8 November)

季
冬
巳
卯
酉
寅
申
子
午
亥
丑
未
戌
辰

Head		VI	
Shoulders	IV		X
Belly	III		IX
Hands	I		VII
Sex		XII	
Knees	II		VIII
Feet	XI		V

季
巳
冬
酉
如
寅
申
亥
午
子
五
未
長
戌

Head		VI	
Shoulders	X		IV
Belly	III		IX
Hands	XII		VII
Sex		I	
Knees	II		VIII
Feet	V		XI

If the sign of the hour of your birth is placed:

on the head of the Yellow Emperor
All your life will pass without care even if your origins are modest, and you will have good luck and a good future; if you are an official you can aspire to the highest ranks. Women of this sign are very stable and can make a good marriage.

on the shoulders
All your life you will be waiting for your opportunity. Sometimes in maturity and above all in old age your destiny can improve. If you do not rely on others and if you are not discouraged by difficulties you can control the outcome. But it is your children above all who will know a better fate.

on the belly
You will have a simple but satisfying life. If you like the arts and music you can attain fame in your mature years. Perhaps then you may become rich. Your happiness and glory will increase with the years.

on the hands
Commerce will be the source of your fortune and your condition of life can greatly improve if you are willing to leave home. Your family will then be abundantly provided for. The beginning of your life will perhaps be modest, but the chances are good that toward the end of your life various riches will accrue from all parts.

on the sex
An assurance of wealth and treasure. At a ripe age you may attain a very important social position. In old age this can only increase and your house will be transformed. No destiny is too high. Your fortune will reflect on your descendants who will be rich and get responsible posts.

on the knees
Your work and your efforts will be in vain. Without being denuded of everything, your life will nevertheless pass in a search that is never satisfied. You are condemned to move on unceasingly. Sometimes, however, you will know a little peace at the end of the road.

on the feet
It will be better if you become a bonze. A peaceful life is necessary to you and you can only find happiness in renunciation. You must avoid living in the house of your ancestors, but you will find peace in wild mountains far from your birthplace. If you are a man you will have two wives; if you are a woman two husbands.

CONCLUSION

All the examples are characteristic of Chinese predictions. Full of verve and popular humour, they must be taken as they have been written down, with something of a smile, when trying to extract from them the information adapted to our own case.

For auspicious and inauspicious indications (notably in relationship with the constellations) I have followed those traditionally given in the calendars, although they are only approximate. Moreover, as we know, they cannot be considered in isolation. Remember the golden rule: no element of a horoscope has any worth in itself but only in its relationship to the whole.

Chapter 17

Relationships between individuals, and between an individual and his activities

RELATIONSHIPS BETWEEN INDIVIDUALS

It is rare for a Chinese to establish his horoscope for purely egotistical reasons. The Chinese, more perhaps than any other race, have always placed great emphasis on social life and on the relationships between individuals. Important occasions, such as a marriage or a business association, necessarily require a more or less detailed comparison between the horoscopes of the two (or more) persons concerned.

If one wishes to make a quick assessment of the chances of understanding between individuals, it is possible to do so by comparing the dominant agents and the animals of the persons concerned.

THE POSSIBILITY OF UNDERSTANDING BETWEEN THE DIFFERENT AGENTS IN CASES OF MARRIAGE OR ASSOCIATIONS

The following list, and there are hundreds of the same sort, is amusing and, moreover, gives an excellent example of the way by which the Chinese understand the relationships of the different Agents.[55] In addition, it completes and specifies the relationship between animals, as we shall see later on. The Agent which is used here as a characteristic of temperament is the one which is associated with the binomial of the year.

N.B. The term 'counterflowing', which we shall use several times below, is a direct translation of the Chinese term. It means that the Agents are placed in reverse order to the normal order of generation: Wood→Fire→Earth→Metal→Water→Wood, etc. . . . In each association, the chief is represented by the man and the associate by the wife.

Man Wood, Woman Wood: When the wind arrives in the forest it breaks wood. The couple will know perpetual disputes, the children will be difficult to bring up and there is a lack of harmony between them.

Man Wood, Woman Fire: Wood engenders Fire. If contradictory subjects are avoided, in spite of occasional disputes, harmony can establish itself and with a little patience happiness comes. Even the Buffalo and the Horse, reputedly incompatible, can in these circumstances succeed in understanding each other. Longevity. Respectful and prosperous offspring.

Man Wood, Woman Earth: Wood dominates the Earth and after the flower comes the fruit. Good understanding between the spouses; money and treasure fill the granary. Few children. It would be desirable for them to undertake charitable work and to live piously.

Man Wood, Woman Metal: Metal destroys Wood, and the man will tend not to stay at home. If he carefully prepares his travels and shows himself charitable, they will know prosperity. Two or three children.

Man Wood, Woman Water: A counterflowing relationship, Water engendering Wood. Relentless work will be needed to achieve prosperity. Preferred choice: agriculture. From two to five children.

Man Fire, Woman Wood: A counterflowing relationship, only half auspicious therefore. If the wife is too strong the husband risks becoming feeble and dying. The family can, however, become prosperous and famous; and the spouses, if they have mutual confidence, can achieve great intimacy. From two to five children.

Man Fire, Woman Fire: A relationship which can become violent, and if they don't take care the couple will see their home become the centre of perpetual storms. However, if one or the other of them is willing to give in the worst will be avoided. They could then have well brought up children.

Man Fire, Woman Earth: Since Fire engenders Earth, this is one of the most auspicious of relationships. The household will be happy and they will have the long life of the pine of the Southern Mountains. The two spouses will efficiently fill their house with treasure. They will have numerous progeny.

Man Fire, Woman Metal: Fire is inauspicious for Metal. In this union the wife is better than her husband. They will have disputes which, if the wife makes no concessions, could lead to serious discord. At the end of their life they risk losing money. If they have sons they must marry strong women.

Man Fire, Woman Water: Water and Fire make an unfavourable union. The spouses can never reach a good understanding. They are mutually jealous and the husband is afraid of his wife. Poverty is to be feared. Three children.

Man Earth, Woman Wood: Earth being high and Wood being low, this conjunction is inauspicious. There will be no harmony in the home where lies and estrangements will develop. Money will grow less, with a risk of shortage. Many badly brought up children.

Man Earth, Woman Fire: Only moderately auspicious because it is a counterflowing relationship. Much human charity will be necessary, but they will not know misery nor serious anxieties. The couple will love each other tenderly. The children will show filial spirit.

Man Earth, Woman Earth: Very harmonious for understanding and feelings. Life begins easily but becomes in time more trying and laborious. If they do not want to be struck down by illness, they must show themselves charitable and pious. The children will not carry on family traditions.

Man Earth, Woman Metal: Earth produces Gold (metal par excellence); money and riches will come to this lucky man. He will live in prosperity and comfort surrounded by many servants. Numerous family, loving wife, all is for the best.

Man Earth, Woman Water: Particularly inauspicious, if the wife lets herself be too influenced by her husband. Misery will follow a glorious beginning. Virtue is most necessary if a peaceable and happy old age is to be achieved. The children will be lacking in affection.

Man Metal, Woman Wood: Metal is hurtful to Wood so this is an inauspicious union. Very difficult start to life, becoming a little better later on. Anxiety over health especially for the two or three children. A little religion will be useful.

Man Metal, Woman Fire: Bad; nothing they undertake will be to their liking. They will know domestic problems and illness all their life. They could have retarded children. In order to redress the situation a little, they should devote themselves to charitable works.

Man Metal, Woman Earth: Counterflowing. The wife wears the trousers and despises her husband. Money will be difficult to keep. It will be necessary to pay strict attention to accounts. The children themselves will be prosperous.

Man Metal, Woman Metal: Dangerous; incessant struggle. After a good enough start the situation deteriorates more and more. The wife is often sick and risks becoming a bigot. Three children.

Man Metal, Woman Water: Extremely prosperous, for Metal engenders Water. All that the man touches will turn to gold. All the wishes of the couple will be realised. Longevity and prosperity assured. Four or six children.

Man Water, Woman Wood: Water engenders Wood; money flows as from a spring. But this facility could lead to a depraved life. If care is taken longevity is assured and life will be peaceful.

Man Water, Woman Fire: Frankly an inauspicious conjunction. The spouses can mutually destroy themselves. Nothing goes well and the family will never have peace. The husband will have a short life. Three to five children.

Man Water, Woman Earth: Counterflowing, not too auspicious. Illness is never absent, goods of all kind are lacking, numerous cares, frequent disputes. It is necessary to correct bad tendencies. Three or four children.

Man Water, Woman Metal: Very auspicious for gold collects on water. Riches abound in the home, the family is surrounded by friends. If they know to whom to give their trust, their prosperity will increase still more. Numerous children.

Man Water, Woman Water: An excess of water indicates uncertainty. Although they are intelligent, their success is not so sure. The spouses do not always agree. In spite of hard work the family stays poor. Five children without filial piety.

I have tried to preserve the flavour of the Chinese text, although the elements of happiness for a traditional Chinese, numerous children, submissive wife, etc., may not strongly commend themselves to a foreigner of this day and age. Nevertheless, I believe that with some slight adaptation these sayings are as applicable to a Westerner as to a Chinese. I have kept the moralising tone, rare enough in horoscopes, because it shows that, in Chinese eyes, free will is the preponderant element in our destiny.

THE POSSIBILITY OF UNDERSTANDING BETWEEN DIFFERENT ANIMALS

This section is brief because this subject has been fully treated in other available books. Don't forget that the indications given below must be completed by consideration of the dominant Agent concerned.[56]

For example, according to his year of birth a Rat can be Metal (*1*, 1924), Water (*13*, 1936), Fire (*25*, 1948), Earth (*37*, 1960), or Wood (*49*, 1972, 1912) while a Dragon can be Wood (*5*, 1928), Metal (*17*, 1940), Water (*29*, 1952), Fire (*41*, 1964) or Earth (*53*, 1976, 1916). This can entirely modify their possible understanding, the affinities being not so complete as it may appear nor the oppositions so total.

1. The **Rat** — Gets on well with Dragon who is the best possible partner for him particularly if the Dragon is a woman; the same goes for the Monkey although he risks not being repaid in kind. Can have no understanding with the Horse, who detests him, nor with the Hare. Agreement with the Goat is difficult but not impossible.

2. The **Buffalo** — Ideal union with a Cock, good understanding with the Snake or perhaps with the Rat, provided this last is truly loving. The Monkey attracts him but he should at any cost avoid him as well as the Goat, the Tiger and the Horse. (However, in connection with his incompatibility with the Horse see the correction for Man Wood, Woman Fire, page 120.)

3. The **Tiger** — Good understanding with the Horse and the Dog but a stormy relationship with the Dragon, which will have an excellent influence on him. Ought not to associate with the Snake or the Buffalo, and ought also to distrust the Monkey, too malignant, and the Hare. Finally, two Tigers cannot live in good understanding with each other. There are some who advise him against the Goat, but I fear that too much is being made of symbolism here.

4. The **Hare** — All goes well in association with the Goat and the Dog; the Pig will have good influence on his moral sense. No understanding with the Cock, the Rat and above all the Tiger. He should avoid the Dragon, who is stronger than he.

5. The **Dragon** — The Dragon gets on well with the Rat, who is in love with him, with the

Cock and the Monkey (the stronger of the two). The male Dragon is attracted by the female Snake. No understanding with the Tiger, the Buffalo and above all the Dog.

6. The **Snake** — Happy with the Cock and the Buffalo if the latter dominates him. Cannot get on with the Tiger or the Pig. Two Snakes cannot live together.

7. The **Horse** — He should find the Goat helpful and the Tiger and the Dog. But he should beware of the Rat, the Monkey and the Buffalo. Two Horses cannot live together.
N.B. Exceptionally for the Horse, the year marked by his own duodenary sign is not auspicious for him.

8. The **Goat** — He gets on well with the Hare, the Pig and the Horse who take him as he comes. He cannot get on with the Rat, and he exasperates the Buffalo and the Dog.

9. The **Monkey** — The Dragon and the Rat can reach an understanding with him but not the Tiger and the Horse. Generally speaking, it is difficult to deal with a Monkey.

10. The **Cock** — Happy with the Buffalo and the Snake but most of all with the Dragon. Nothing in common with the Hare, little understanding with the Dog. Two Cocks cannot live under the same roof.

11. The **Dog** — Can find happiness with the Horse and the Tiger who supports him, but above all with the Hare with whom he will find peace. No possible understanding with the Dragon, the Goat and the Cock.

12. The **Pig** — Good understanding with the Hare and the Goat who will know how to lead him. No luck with the Snake or the Monkey.

In brief. For every animal, generally speaking and save for the exceptions which have been mentioned, the relationships are the same as those of the signs they are connected with. See charts on page 79.

HOW TO ASSESS THE RELATIONSHIPS BETWEEN AN INDIVIDUAL AND HIS ACTIVITIES AND EVENTS GENERALLY

The Chinese believe that the astrological forces which influence the destiny of the World and political and social events are different from those which rule individual destinies. The Chinese, knowing their personal horoscopes, consult almanacs which give general influences whenever they want to embark on some important venture.

However, it is possible for us to discover whether or not a year, a month, a day or even an hour may be favourable by referring to the tables of affinities and antipathies between signs (Chapter 11), between agents (Chapter 12 and earlier in this chapter) and between animals (above).

To give a simple example: for any animal the year is favourable whose duodenary sign is identical or in harmony with its own sign. The year is unfavourable if the sign is in opposition. In any other case the influences are neutral. There are two exceptions: for the Horse and the Cock the year of their own duodenary sign is not favourable.

Chapter 18

Summary and examples

From all that has been said, it is now possible for us to conclude that in China the calculation of the eight signs of our destiny obeys laws as precise as those of the Western horoscope. Moreover the eight signs are easier to use; and the conversion of Western dates to the Chinese system requires little effort compared with the calculation of sidereal time and the position of the stars in the sky in the Western horoscope. Of course for a Chinese it is easier still because the eight signs are written down for him on the day of his birth.

If you wish to master this system of divination to the fullest extent, a complete understanding of the content of this book is indispensable. We can now summarise the procedure necessary for casting a horoscope.

1. To establish our eight signs of destiny

This preliminary process is the necessary basis for every divinatory operation; the method is given on page 61 and the pages following. For more details refer:

for the year page 61 (remember that the duodenary sign is the most significant sign).

for the month page 62 (remember that the duodenary sign is the most significant sign).

for the day page 72 (remember that the denary sign is the most significant sign).

for the hour page 73 (the duodenary sign is the most important).

To find the two signs relevant to each time, refer to the table on page 74.

N.B. 1. In China the lunar year (peasant year) begins on a date which varies between 21 January and 20 February (see tables, pages 64–67). It is this date on which are calculated the horoscopic works of Vietnamese inspiration based on the twelve animals; but Chinese traditional astrologers prefer to reckon the astrological year from the day of 'the Establishment of Spring', 4 or 5 February (pages 68–71).

2. To convert time to that of the meridian of Peking, remember that Peking time is eight hours ahead of Greenwich Mean Time (GMT). Depending on where you were born, add or subtract the appropriate number of hours.

2. To study the temperament

This is above all based on the Five Agents; on their association with the binomial, see page 84, with the denary signs, see page 86, and with the duodenary signs, see page 88. Once the Five Agents have been found, their relationships (page 82) and their interpretation (page 90, et seq.) must be studied.

In general, the Agent associated with the binomial of the year gives the dominant factor of your temperament, while the Agent associated with the binomial of the day determines primarily the factor of luck.

The Agents thus appear twelve times in your horoscope (page 93).

3. Study of the moral character by the twelve animals

(For their meaning, page 30, et seq., and interpretation, page 97, et seq.)

The animal for the year should be studied in association with the duodenary cycle (page 88 and table, page 97). You can complete the study by a comparison with the animal associated with the duodenary sign of the hour of birth.

4. The factor of luck

1. A more simple method: by comparison of your constellation of birth (how to find it, page 103; its significance, page 104, et seq.) with the Agent associated with the binomial of your birthday.

2. A more complicated traditional method: by comparing the relationship between
the duodenary sign of the month of birth (and associated Agent)
the denary sign of the birthday (and associated Agent)
the binomial of the hour of birth (and associated Agents).

5. Sympathies and antipathies, compatibilities and incompatibilities

Compare the animals (indication given for each of them on page 97, et seq.) and the Agents (page 90, et seq.) of the two people concerned. Although the examples referred to deal with relationships between husband and wife, it is easy to transpose them for other relationships, such as business partnerships, etc. . . . If (as for the Agents) a hierarchy is indicated the husband is regarded as the most important partner.

6. Auspicious and inauspicious days

Having found the constellation of the day (calculation, page 103; interpretation, page 104, et seq.) and the Agent associated with the binomial of the day (page 84), comparison with the Agent dominating your birthday will allow you to relate the diagnosis to yourself. You can also consult the list on page 120 et seq.

These are just a few examples of the different ways of using the eight signs of your destiny and their affinities. The list is not exhaustive and you are free to think of others. The only criterion for the Chinese lies in the quality of the result obtained from them.

CASE HISTORIES

Finally I give examples of two persons I know, and how I worked out their horoscopes step by step by way of illustrating all that we have discussed in this book.

First example

A woman born in London on 10 August 1948 at 11.15 a.m.

Assemble the data

1st Step Find the numbers of the four binomials

(a) *for the year* (see page 61) 1948 minus 3 divided by 60, the remainder is 25. So the year comes under the 25th binomial.

(b) *for the month* (see page 62) 10 August falls within the 7th month which begins on 7 August (if we want to follow the lunar calendar, see chart on page 63. Here the 7th month starts on 5 August, so for our present purpose there is no difference.). From page 62 we can see that in any year ending with an 8, months start with the 51st binomial; the 7th month therefore comes under the 57th binomial.
(c) *for the day* (see page 71) We see that 10 August (in a leap year) is the 223rd day of the year. As we see from the chart, we must add 21 which gives 244. Divide by 60 and the remainder is 4. So the day comes under the 4th binomial.
(d) *for the hour* (see page 72) As the binomial of the day is the 4th, the first hour of the day is marked by the 37th binomial. The hour of birth 11.15 will be 19.15 in Peking and falls within the eleventh two-hour period. The hour of birth therefore comes under the 47th binomial.

2nd Step Constellation of the day of birth (see page 103)
To find the constellation of the day, bear in mind the number of the day in the year which, as we have seen, is 223. According to the table we must add 7 which gives 230. Divide by 28 and the remainder is 6, which is the number of the constellation, the Tail, which falls on Tuesday.

3rd Step Find the eight signs and the Agents (see chart, page 84)
According to the relevant binomial number, we see that under the binomial of the year (25) the denary sign is 戊 *Wu* (a–5) and the duodenary 子 *Tzŭ* (α–I); under the month (57) the denary sign is 庚 *Keng* (g–7) and the duodenary 申 *Shen* (ι–IX); under the day (4) the denary sign is 丁 *Ting* (d–4) and the duodenary 卯 *Mao* (δ–IV); under the hour (47) the denary sign is 庚 *Keng* (g–7) and the duodenary 戌 *Hsü* (λ–XI).

From the same chart we see that the Agents for the year are: 火 Fire, associated with the binomial 25, 土 Earth, associated with the denary sign and 水 Water, associated with the duodenary sign. In the same way, we see that for the month (binomial 57) we have respectively: 木 Wood, 金 Metal and 金 Metal. For the day (binomial 4) we have 火 Fire, 火 Fire and 木 Wood. For the hour (binomial 47), we have 金 Metal, 金 Metal and 土 Earth.

4th Step Find the animals (see page 97)
Many people take only the animal of the year into account. We think it advisable to consider also the animal of the hour. In this case the animal of the year (1948) is Rat, and the animal of the hour (11th period) is Dog.

5th Step The Emperor's body (see page 112)
Find the duodenary sign of the hour (*Hsü* 戌 λ–XI) on the Emperor's body. According to Chinese ideas the 10 August falls in the beginning of autumn; so we can see that *Hsü* 戌 in this case is placed on the Emperor's knee.

INTERPRETATION

1 The Factor of Luck

In assessing the luck of an individual, we first consider the constellation of the day. In this case, the constellation, the Tail, is a lucky one (see page 105) for it ensures success in any enterprise and for the family. On the other hand, the indications given by the Emperor's body (see page 118) suggest that the subject will face difficulties. She should be successful in the end but only after a struggle.

The Chinese believe that the Agents of the binomial of the year and of the day affect the luck of an individual. The subject's Agent of the year is Fire, 'Fire at the foot of the hill', which, in this case, is the symbol of achievement, but in a discreet way. Since Fire is also the Agent of the day, 'Fire of the furnace', the prospects of achievement are as good as they possibly can be, but in a domestic kind of way. The fact that the subject was born in the first quarter of the moon is also a good omen.

2 Character Sketch

In order to assess the subject's character, it is necessary to consider all the signs and Agents as a whole. Each individual element can only be understood in the context of its relationships with the others. In the subject's case, all five Agents are represented: 4 Metals, 3 Fires, 2 Woods, 1 Water and 2 Earth. This in itself is good because her character has a firm basis on which to develop. The only reservation we have here is that the subject is over-endowed with will power (4 Metals) and a little short of lucidity (1 Water). She would do well, therefore, to associate with people whose tally of agents complements hers, e.g. with someone who is more lucid and more flexible. It is worth emphasising at this point that this combination of Agents is the main key to the subject's character and all other factors must be considered with this in mind.

The proportion of *Yin* and *Yang* are 3 *Yang* and 1 *Yin*. This, for a woman, indicates a slight lack of feminity in comportment. The balance is partly redressed, however, by her two animals which are *Yin*.

There are no oppositions in the subject's binomials and no weakness in their composition. The duodenary signs of the year and the month have an affinity, and the duodenary signs of the day and hour are in sympathy with each other. This suggests a strong character divided equally between her outer self (year and month) and inner self (day and hour).

3 Detailed Study of the Character

Let us consider first the binomials of the year and the month because they seem to be especially linked. In the subject's case these portray her outer self. They indicate a firm equilibrium as all the Agents are represented and in particular Metal/Will Power appears twice. From this we deduce complete self control. Earth/Realism appears only in the denary sign of the year and manifests itself in sensible behaviour. In the binomial of the year, the duodenary sign is the more important. In this case Water is counterflowing to Earth: this is unnatural but the presence of Fire reestablishes a kind of stability as it strengthens Earth. This means that patience, sensibility and realism are well balanced. In the binomial of the month, however, we find that Metal/Will Power, repeated twice, has a firm but possibly excessive grasp on creativity.

The general picture of the subject so far is one of a well endowed personality whose qualities are not too apparent on account of an excessive control over her actions.

Let us now consider the binomial of the day in conjunction with the binomial of the hour. As we have seen, they are strongly connected and give an idea of the subject's inner self. This inner self is dangerously lacking in realism. The denary sign of the day, Fire, which is also the Agent of the binomial of the day, strongly indicates passion. But since the binomial is *Yin*, this passion is introverted and possibly possessive. It is not much affected by action and creativity (Wood). In the binomial of the hour, which is *Yang*, we find strong will (Metal twice) and Earth which reinforces the will and may add a touch of realism. Here the association of the day and hour binomials gives a good equilibrium between *Yin* and *Yang*. But if will and passion are concentrated on one object, a dangerous situation may emerge because the outer appearance of self control may not be strong enough to check her determination to achieve her ends.

In considering how the animals affect the subject's character, we need only refer to page 97 and what it says about the Rat which is born under the sign of *charm*. The apparent calm of those born in the year of the Rat disguises their strength and toughness. This confirms what we have already seen. The subject's animal of the day is the Dog (page 101) and this means that she has the qualities of loyalty, honesty and common sense but is subject to anxiety. She is a bit of a conformist and inspires confidence. She may have a propensity to pessimism and to seeing the black side of things. Her lucidity combined with anxiety, in spite of a warm nature, makes it difficult for her to be happy in love.

She would do well to associate with people born in the year of the Dragon (see page 99) and the Monkey (page 101) but not with those born in the year of the Horse (page 100) or, to a lesser extent, the Goat (page 100) and the Hare (page 99). But we must remember that these comparisons should be completed by comparisons with the Agents of the binomials of the year of the persons concerned, which may throw quite a different light on these relationships. In fact, to make a true assessment of the potential relationships between two people, we must compare their full horoscopes.

Second Example

Horoscope of a man born in Paris on 14 March 1934 at 8 a.m.

1 Establishment of the theme

(a) First, find the four binomials

– of the year	the eleventh	B	*Yang*	
– of the month	the fourth	C	*Yin*	(lunation or period)
– of the day	the twenty-first	D	*Yang*	
– of the hour	the ninth	B	*Yang*	(Peking time)

(b) Second, find the eight signs

– of the year	1	XI
– of the month	4	IV
– of the day	1	IX
– of the hour	9	IX

(c) Third, find the Agents

	binomial	denary sign	duodenary sign
– of the year	Fire	Wood	Earth
– of the month	Fire	Fire	Wood
– of the day	Water	Wood	Metal
– of the hour	Metal	Water	Metal

(d) Fourth, find the Animal
– of the year 1934: DOG.
– of the hour (ninth Chinese hour): MONKEY.

(e) Fifth, find the Constellation of the birthday
– seventh Constellation, the Basket, which falls on a Wednesday, auspicious.

(f) Sixth, find the factor of chance of the hour of birth
By Chinese reckoning, 14 March comes in the middle of Spring and sign IV is placed on the right foot of the Yellow Emperor.

(g) Seventh, find the phase of the Moon
In 1934, the second lunation began on 13 March; we are therefore near the beginning of the third quarter.

2 Study of the aspects of the astrological theme

Proportion of Yin *and* Yang. Three out of four binomials are *Yang* which, for a man, is an excellent proportion, particularly when the year and the day are both *Yang*. Any excess in this proportion is modified by the fact that the Dog is *Yin* as well as the Monkey (though with less emphasis).

Relationship between the signs and the binomials. No important opposition between the signs, while the opposition which could eventually appear between the outer self and the strongly marked inner self (the day and the hour are linked by duodenary sign IX) is corrected by the fact that denary sign I appears in both the binomial of the day and that of the year. The binomial of the day is weak, but this fault is compensated for by the fact that the binomial of the day is reinforced by that of the hour.

Role of the Five Agents. All five Agents are present and this is an important factor for equilibrium. Fire (three) dominates the year and the month (the social aspect of the personality). Metal (three) dominates the hour and the day (the deeper aspect of the personality). A superficially exuberant nature, but obstinate and tough underneath. Realism indicated by Earth (one) is rather weak, but imagination and creativity are strong. The presence of the auspicious denary sign in Spring is extremely auspicious for the hour of birth.

3 The factor of chance
Constellation 7 is auspicious and brings success mainly in business. The hour of birth suggests that the subject is basically a solitary person and that it would be better if he lived far from his parents.
The Agent which presides over the binomial of the year 'Fire on the mountain' could indicate a striking success, while that of the binomial of the day 'Water of springs and wells' seems to bring domestic happiness.

4 Study of the character
The subject can count on good fortune, which seems almost excessive. The image he conveys

is that of an exuberant nature, but the absence of Water in the outer self and the presence of only one Earth suggests a certain lack of realism and efficiency.

In contrast with the passionate aspect of the social self, the inner self is cold and obstinate. If these traits develop, they can become hard and calculating. Disguised in every day life, the subject's obstinate determination is a characteristic which others must take into account.

There is no real opposition between the Animal of the day, the Dog, and that of the hour, the Monkey, although the general disdain which the Monkey feels for other animals can indicate a dissatisfaction of the inner self with his social life. The Dog is an honest and loyal, though slightly anxious, animal while the Monkey is a calculating, egotistical animal who can always get what he wants.

The chances of success are excellent provided that he can control his 'daemon within'.

Understanding. An association with the Horse and the Tiger will be beneficial to him, but most of all with the Hare. No possibility of understanding with the Dragon, the Goat or the Cock.

CONCLUSION

As you can see, the interpretation of a horoscope is a very personal matter for which there are no true rules. This is why my examples have been presented in a fairly succint manner, though detailed enough to show the reader how to proceed.

To find out the more or less auspicious times for the first subject, for example, those periods dominated by Fire or Wood (which gives birth to Fire) are the most favourable, while those dominated by Water are less so. The other periods are neutral, but since all the Agents are present in her horoscope, no periods can affect her significantly.

The various data of a horoscope should always be taken in the context of the whole and not separately. Thus, when I studied the factor of chance in the first horoscope, I did not emphasise the connection between the sign of the hour and the season, although it was clearly unfavourable, as, in the second horoscope, was the weak aspect (D) of the binomial of the day. In each case the other factors of the horoscope corrected and, in a way, neutralised these aspects. Finally, we must remember that a horoscope does not give a definitive picture. The circumstances of a person's life, his relationships with those about him, his environment and his profession can prevent some tendencies from developing or, on the other hand, help others to acquire too great a relative importance. A horoscope describes the profile of a character with its strong and weak points; and the Chinese believe that, by doing so, it helps a person to develop his latent possibilities and to correct his faults.

Conclusion

You are now in possession of the eight signs of your destiny. At first sight perhaps the process may have seemed somewhat complicated because of the strangeness of the Chinese calendar, but in fact it is less difficult than the computing of Western horoscopes.

The definition of time by means of the four cycles of sixty groups of signs is used in an identical manner by all the peoples whose culture was based, at least in the beginning, on the same written tradition and on ideograms: China, Korea, Vietnam and Japan (although since the MEIJI Era the Japanese have tried to adapt the cycles to a Western style calendar).

The Chinese year begins officially on the first day of the first moon of Spring, called 'Passing of the Year' or 'Spring Festival'. The present rulers of China, having adopted the Western New Year, have only kept the second name, as having fewer religious implications than the first one.

In China the first day of the year is used for calculating a person's age. A child from the moment of birth is considered to be one year old, and after the following New Year, even if only one day has passed, two years old. If, therefore, you are told that a child is a 'Rat' you can deduce that he was five or seventeen years old in 1977; but if you are told that he is six years old it means in fact that he is only four or five years old.

The Calendar used by Chinese astrologers is the solar calendar which begins with the 'Establishment of Spring' (4 or 5 February) as the starting point of the 'genethliacal' astrological cycle. A few, however, stick to the Lunar New Year, the 'Spring Festival', the first day of the first lunar month. Obviously we must not confuse 'Spring Festival' with 'Establishment of Spring'.

If the method of calculating the signs of destiny is uniform and consistent, the same is not true for their interpretation which for thousands of years has given rise to many diverse commentaries, often contradictory, from innumerable schools of thought and traditions. Such riches are no worry to the Chinese who are incorrigible optimists and who, as far as possible, would be willing to try them all. In much the same way a Chinese who needs medical attention is ready to use simultaneously the prescriptions of several practitioners, both Western and traditional: after all one never knows . . . The Chinese are essentially tolerant; they never exclude nor condemn. In such matters there is no question of a true method or a false one; at the most, by use, perhaps one might be found better than another.

I am reminded at this point of a parable much appreciated by the Chinese: that of the three blind men and the elephant. Three blind men were talking among themselves about what an elephant was. Unable to agree they groped around until finally they found one. Each of them touched a different part: one touched the foot, another the trunk and another the belly. In the discussion which followed each thought that his experience proved, in the case of the first blind man, that the elephant was just like a column; 'like a tube' said the second; 'no', said the third, 'it is like the roof of a tent'. Their error, of course, was to assume the whole from knowledge of only one part. 'In my Father's House there are many mansions' and there are numerous paths that lead to enlightenment.

The eight signs are not designed to help a fortune teller in looking into the future. In Chinese eyes this would be the equivalent of using a steam hammer to crack a nut. There are simpler methods to find a reply to a precise question. But the signs are meant to help us bring out general characteristics of a personality in a more and more precise manner as our insight grows deeper. In a way they are the material support which make concentration of mind possible: rather like the 'mandalas', those geometrical figures sprinkled with coloured powders which help Tibetan sages to concentrate and then to attain the mental vacuity and absence of all sensual perception necessary for contemplation.

When a prediction is too inauspicious, one does not admit defeat but looks instead for a new interpretation, based on the slightest favourable indication that may not yet have been discovered. A Chinese never confesses himself definitely beaten; he will try to the very last to find a way of cheating fate. I remember one day in Saigon I was brought a piece of yellow printed paper which had been found stuck on the door of one of the Counsellors of the High Commission. It was thought to be a signal for a secret meeting or an attack on the house. In fact, the paper was concerned with a worrying prediction about the illness of a young child. Unable to burn the paper at the risk of enhancing its power, the mother had no doubt thought to divert the bad luck to some 'foreign devil'.

In my explanation of the eight signs which are so steeped in Chinese folklore, I wish to make clear that I stuck closely enough to the texts to preserve their colour. As our vision of the world surprises and often shocks the Chinese, so theirs with good reason often leads us astray, above all their indifference to systems of thought which in our view are perfectly arranged and logical. But in an age which proclaims the necessity for ecumenism, while retaining its prejudices and intolerance, should we not try to realise the life and warmth of humanity in a different context?

As with acupuncture, the true source of interpretation of oracles is innumerable sayings in verse which are often obscure and require the help of an expert. They contain old oral traditions which we now find written down in almanacks and many little manuals of divination. It is these traditions, necessarily condensed, which have inspired me here.

I should like to emphasise, in a comparison that I have already used, that these eight signs are like eight playing cards which you hold in your hand; none has any value by itself but only in relation to the other seven. Even then the outcome of the game cannot be taken for granted, for it depends on the play of the others taking part and on your own skill in making use of your cards. There are in the world thousands of Mozarts who are smothered by their environment or hampered by the poor use they can make of their natural gifts: even the best of hands can be spoilt.

Another very characteristic reaction is to distrust instinctively too great a slice of luck for, as we know, extremes have a tendency to turn into their own opposites. I have known Mahjong players to ruin their games deliberately because they have been given too good a hand. All excess is a fault and too fine a horoscope should make one pause for it departs from the middle way and is not human. A diviner will give no pleasure to a Chinese if he tells him only good things for he will be suspected of flattery or partiality.

NOTES

INTRODUCTION

The description given in this book of Chinese divination by means of the eight signs is a serious work based on a careful study of many Chinese texts; but a detailed list of my sources, useful as it might be to a sinologue, would go far beyond the scope of this book. I give brief references to my sources only when they are necessary for the understanding or justification of my argument.

Chinese sources

For classical texts, the *Thirteen Canonical Books*, 十三經 published by the World Publishing Company, 世界書局 *Shih Chieh Shu Chü*, Shanghai. The most important of them for my purpose was the 易經 *I Ching* 'Book of Changes'.

For all the works of the Chinese 'Sages' (子 *tzŭ*, often translated as philosopher, but this is not strictly accurate for they were not creators of philosophical systems of thought), I have referred to the collection 諸子集成 , *Chu Tzŭ Chi Ch'eng*, also published by the World Publishing Company. This collection includes two separate commentaries on the 道德經 *Tao Te Ching*, the 'Book of the Way and its Virtue', and to the collection 四部備要 , *Ssŭ Pu Pei Yao*, published by the China Publishing Company, 中華書局 , *Chung Hua Shu Chü*, Shanghai, including in particular the 黃帝內經素問 , *Huang Ti Nei Ching Su Wen*, 'Colloquy on Medicine of the Yellow Emperor' by an unknown author. The text seems to have reached its present form in the second century BC. This book is generally referred to as the *Nei Ching*.

I have also consulted Chinese almanacks of the past thirty years, and a large number of little manuals of divination and acupuncture, which I refer to individually when it is necessary. I have not thought it worthwhile to give a detailed bibliography of Chinese sourçes, since Needham's work (see the following paragraph) contains an unrivalled list.

Western sources

Although I have consulted most of the works of Western Sinologues which have a bearing on my subject, most of them are inadequate and I have made few references to them, as only two were really useful to me. First, the monumental and still not fully published *Science and Civilisation in China* by Joseph Needham, Cambridge University Press. Happily for me, the most essential parts for my work have appeared, in particular Volume II (1956) 'History of Scientific Thought' and Volume III (1959) 'Mathematics. The Science of the Heaven and Earth'. In addition to the quality of his text, his notes and his detailed bibliography have helped me to find easily essential Chinese sources, thus sparing me hours of research. Second, on the Chinese calendar itself, the fundamental work is 'Notes concernant la chronologie chinoise' by the Reverend Fathers Havret and Chambeau, and published in *Variétés Sinologiques* No. 52, Shanghai, 1922. This essentially practical work, if a little too dense, is still the standard basic text, although the important distinction between the solar and lunar calendars is never clearly made (but nor do any of the other sinologues do so), and I have had to revise their astronomical calculations.

NOTES

1 I have translated the word 經 *ching* as book. No translation is really satisfactory for the word originally meant a canal bearing water and was applied to all books which were sources of enlightenment and moral conduct. In acupuncture, this term is used for 'canals' linking the points through which energy circulates and which Western acupuncturists obstinately call 'meridians', as absurd a designation as the use of the word 'elements' for the Five Agents which are likewise sources of energy (see Chapter 12 p. 82 and especially Chapter 7 p. 33 of this book).

2 See Introduction to Notes 'Western sources'.

3 'The name that can be named is not the everlasting name' (see p. 9 of this book).

4 Confucius, *Analects*, Book XII ch. XI, translated by James Legge in *The Chinese Classics* Vol. I, p. 240, 2nd revised edition, Oxford, Clarendon Press, 1893.

5 The whole of the classic 中庸, *Chung Yung*, is an expression of the doctrine of the Golden Mean. Legge op. cit., Vol. I, p. 382.

6 There are many commentaries on the *Tao Te Ching* and, as I have indicated above (p. 9), many translations. Legge, *The Texts of Taoism*, Oxford 1891, Vol. 2; Wieger, *Les Pères du Système Taoiste* Hien-hien 1913. Ch'u Ta-Kao, *Tao Te Ch'ing*, Allen & Unwin, London 1959; Blakney, *The Way of Life*, New York 1955; Duyvendak, *Tao Tö King*, Paris 1953; Liou Kia-Hway *Tao Tö King*, Paris 1967, etc.

This book is attributed to a little known personage whose history has been obscured by an inextricable web of myths and fables: 老子 Lao Tzŭ, the 'old Master' par excellence. Compared with the moralising and down to earth pragmatism of the Confucian tradition, the mystical verve of Lao Tzŭ and his chief disciple, Chuang Tzŭ, is invigorating. Despite the relentlessness with which most of its translators have tried to find a philosophical system in the *Tao Te Ching*, I see in it rather a poetic and mystical attempt to apprehend the Universe. Unfortunately, the wisdom which informs Lao Tzŭ's work has degenerated into a nebulous system encumbered with superstition and magic. Lao Tzŭ is no more responsible than Christ or Buddha for the utterances and contradictions of many of their followers.

The picture on p. 9 expresses very well the intimate and harmonious relationship which the Sage should find with nature: this is the essence of true Taoism. The recent discovery (December 1973) at Ch'angsha, in a tomb of the Han dynasty dating from the second century BC, of the two oldest known examples of Lao Tzŭ's work led to the publication in 1981 of a critical edition which has made some important changes necessary to the text known hitherto. This is why I have preferred the word 恒, *heng* (the fifth and eleventh ideograms in my quotation from Lao Tzŭ). In place of 常, *ch'ang*, which has been substituted on account of a taboo: *heng* figured in the name of the Emperor *Wen* 文 (179 BC.) For a discussion of this kind of taboo see page 24.

Although the two ideograms are practically synonymous, *heng* seems to me to express the idea of uninterrupted continuity more clearly than *ch'ang* which can mean frequent repetition.

7 This diagram of two interlaced figures is extremely popular in China for it is the most evocative expression of the duality, *Yin* and *Yang*. Accordingly one finds it reproduced everywhere in the decorations of temples, magical emblems and writings, the signs of secret societies, etc. The origin of the diagram is obscure. Werner, in his *Myths and Legends of China*, London, 1922, thinks that its creator was 周敦頤 Chou Tun-Yi, AD 1017–73, a celebrated scholar who gave a new stimulus to Confucian thought. 'By his famous *T'ai Chi T'u*, or Diagram of the Great Origin (or Grand Terminus),' he shows, 'that the Grand Original Cause, itself uncaused, produces the *Yang* and the *Yin*, these the five elements (sic), and so on, through the male and female norms *(tao)*, to the production of all things,' p. 86.

Personally I tend to think that the diagram must be of older, Taoist origin and is not the expression of a philosophical idea but a symbol of the evolution of everything in the world. The process is illustrated as follows:

From the unknowable 道, *Tao*, emanates the first Principle 太乙, *T'ai I*, which is expressed in 太極, *T'ai Chi*, the first division into a dualism containing *Yin* and *Yang*. From *T'ai Chi* is derived: in terms of energy, the five agents and all their associated forces; in terms of numerology (see p. 47), the first pair *Yin* and *Yang*, the four dual combinations ⚌, ⚍, ⚎, ⚏, the eight trigrams (see p. 12) and the 64 hexagrams of the I Ching. These are two distinct but complementary systems.

These terms *T'ai Yi* and *T'ai Chi* have been misunderstood by some Western authorities. *T'ai Yi* is translated as 'Great Unity, the nest egg of evolution' by Baller (Chinese-English Dictionary, Shanghai 1900, p. 436) and by Mathews as 'The great Monad from which all things sprang' (Chinese-English Dictionary, Shanghai 1931, p. 860). These definitions are a good illustration of how difficult it is to translate a non-philosophic Chinese thought into Western concepts. While accepting the general idea of the principle of evolution, I cannot agree with their definitions for it seems to me that they contradict the meaning of the ideogram *Yi*. This ideogram which we know well, is in fact the second of the denary signs and signifies 'second'.

Moreover, if we consider the matter etymologically (see p. 26) the first stage in the development of a bud is 甲 *chia*, an excellent illustration of the beginning of evolution; whereas 乙 *yi* is the second stage in which a sprout leaves the bud, a symbol of blossoming.

Instead of translating *T'ai Chi t'u* as 'diagram of the absolute, why not translate *T'ai Chi T'u* as a mere definition of the diagram: 'Diagram of the (two) poles'? In this way we do not misconstrue Chinese grammar which has no mark to indicate the plural such as 's' in English. Thus, instead of an abstract philosophical term, we have a diagram of the stages of evolution.

8 See pictures on pp. 40 and 59.

9 莊子 *Chuang Tzŭ*, Ch. 21, translated by Dr L. Wieger *Taoïsme* Vol. 2, 'Les Pères du Système Taoiste' Hsien-hsien, 1913, p. 383.

10 As shown in all Chinese communist texts, such as those of *Liu Shao-chi Lin Piao*, and especially *Mao Tse-tung* in his numerous writings, notably the 'Little Red Book'.

11 See Van Gulik *Sexual Life in ancient China*, Leiden, 1962.

12 The arrangement of the trigrams around the *T'ai Chi* is the traditional one. There are other magical and esoteric diagrams, where the trigrams are arranged differently.

13 The 'tortoise' represents the most ancient form of divination, as attested by the oracle bones (1300 BC). The method of divination is to heat tortoise shells or scapular bones of buffalo until they crack. The shape of the cracks give an answer, yes or no, to the question asked. Hence the shape of the ideogram 卜 *pu*, 'divination' which represents the cracks made in this way.

The 'milfoil', or rather the twigs or sticks of milfoil, are still used to this day for consulting the hexagrams of the *I Ching*, by dividing a bunch of fifty sticks according to a particular rite (see Blofeld *I Ching* London, 1965, p. 62).

14 書經 *Shu Ching*, 'The great Plan', Part V, Book IV, 25, translated by James Legge, op. cit. Vol. III, part II, p. 337.

15 書經 *Shu Ching*, Part I, Book II, chapter II, 18, translated by Legge, op. cit. Vol. III, part I, p. 63.

16 As ancient texts seem to indicate, Earth clearly marks the return to the Centre at the end of each season (see p. 17 and 36 of this book), particularly at the end of summer when, in the cycle of the agents, Fire gives birth to Earth. This is why the dog days, which mark the end of summer for the Chinese, are especially dedicated to Earth. This is the time when the monsoon brings humidity and fertility to North China. See 命學入門, *Ming Hsüeh ju men*, by 段方, *Tuan Fang*, 'Introduction to Divination' Taiwan, 1969, p. 59; see also *Pao p'u tzŭ* op. cit. p. 20.

17 Commentary of the *Nei Ching*, chapter 66, op. cit. p. 136.

18 The cycle of Jupiter of 12 years dominates the cycle of 60 years, 元 *yüan*, and that of three *yüan* (三元) of 180 years, 15 cycles of Jupiter.

It is interesting to note that the cycle of 180 years is very close to the cycle of 179 years at the end of which the Jupiter effect occurs. At the end of each cycle of 179 years the five principal planets are in conjunction and have the maximum influence on Earth. See *The Jupiter Effect* by John Gribbin and Stephen H. Plagemann. The present Chinese cycle ends in 1983; the cycle of 179 years ends in 1982.

19 Havret & Chambeau op. cit. p. 26.

20 四柱 *Ssŭ chu* are the four binomials, 'pillars' of destiny, one each for the year, the month, the day and the hour, while the 八字, pa tzŭ the eight signs, are the eight ideograms of which the binomials are composed. The two terms are interchangeable: the literati prefer the four pillars but eight signs is the popular usage. See Lister, *Marco Polo's travels in Xanadu with Kublai Khan*, London, 1976, pp. 100 and 101.

21 It is interesting to note that maintaining the secrecy of the personal name is widely practised. Speaking about India, Louis Chochod in his *Occultisme et Magie en Extreme Orient*, Paris, Payot, 1945, p. 52 says: 'The infant receives two names of which one remains secret and is known only by his parents. This precaution is taken to prevent curses being directed at the child by an enemy. The true name is the one known only by the parents and, later, by the child concerned. The common name is merely a pseudonym against which a curse would be useless. *Note:* A similar belief is still current amongst the Annamites.'

22 See C. P. Fitzgerald's *China*, Barrie and Jenkins, 4th edition, 1976, p. 20, et seq. The ideograms of the denary cycle figure in nearly all inscriptions associated with dates and names of royal ancestors.

23 On the origin of the cyclic ideograms, see Needham op. cit. Vol. III, p. 396, et seq., and on their use in divination see ibid. Vol. II, p. 357, et seq. On this inversion see Granet op. cit. pp. 154, 155.

For the etymology of the cyclic ideograms, see 說文解字 *Shuo wen chieh tzŭ*, by 許真 *Hsü Shen* (121 AD), which is the source for Dr L. Wieger S.J. in his *Chinese Characters*, Peking Edition Henri Vetch, reissue, 1940. I have also made great use of the work of Karlgren *Analytical Dictionary of Chinese and Sino-Japanese*, Paris 1923, and *Gramatica Senica*, Gothenberg 1940, and of the Dictionary of forms of Divinatory inscriptions 甲古文篇, *Chia Ku Wen Tien*.

As my purpose here is simply to study the divinatory tradition, I have not thought it necessary to give all the ancient forms of ideograms nor the varied and often fanciful explanations of Chinese scholars.

24 For the explanations given here concerning the cyclic animals, I have largely followed the excellent and remarkable book *A Cycle of Chinese Festivities* by C. S. Wong, Singapore 1967, a work rather dense but very serious and well documented. As far as I know, Mr Wong's study on the twelve animals is the most complete there is. The abundance and precision of his documentation has been extremely useful to me. During a recent visit to China (November 1981) my attention was drawn to the fact that the cycle of the twelve animals was in use in the beginning of the T'ang dynasty. They appear on a very beautiful stone discovered near Sian in a recently excavated tomb of the T'ang Princess, Chang Huai, who died in the seventh century AD.

25 Needham op. cit. Vol. II p. 216, et seq., Manfred Porket in *The Theoretical Foundations of Chinese Medicine*, London, 1979, speaks of the 'Five Evolutive Phases (p. 45, et seq.). Du Bary in *Sources of Chinese Tradition* Columbia University Press, 1964 used the appellation 'Five Agents', p. 198. Blofeld in *Gateway to Wisdom*, Allen & Unwin, 1980 uses the term 'Five Activities'.

26 See Lavier, Jacques, *L'Acupuncture chinoise, Tchou*, Paris 1966, p. 118, et seq. (see note 15 supra).

27 The Chinese have two dissimilar terms for Earth; Earth as opposed to Sky is called 地 *ti*, while earth (or soil) is called 土 *t'u*.

28 This diagram is given in the 難經 *Nan Ching (Ssŭ Pu Pei Yao* op. cit. Vol. 65, p. 5) a work complementary to the *Nei Ching*, whose difficulties it explains. The Chinese believe that there is a biorythm adapted to the organs of the body, in the course of the year, the day and the hour. Instead of the month, acupuncturists in this case take the period of a denary cycle.

29 *Nei Ching*, op. cit., ch. 67. *Pao p'u tzŭ*, op. cit., p. 70.

30 Pictures taken from 近代秘密社會史料, *Chin Tai Mi Mi Shih Hui Shih Liao*, 'Historical data on Contemporary Secret Societies', Peking 1935. Centre of Historical researches of the Peip'ing National Institute, ch. 6, p. 35.

31 The 月令 *Yüeh Ling* (a chapter of the *Li Chi* see p. 5 of this book) mentions nearly all these constellations. The complete list is found in the 淮南子鴻烈解, *Huai Nan Tzŭ hung lieh chieh*, 'The book of the Prince of Huai nan' BC 120.

I have had to check the chart of the 28 Constellations very carefully. Needham (op. cit., III p. 232, et seq.) is content to give the position of the significant stars of each constellation. His map is not precise enough to allow other stars to be identified. Havret & Chambeau (op. cit.) have no map.

The list contained in the Chinese-French Dictionary of Couvreur, p. 1074, and the Chinese-English Dictionaries of Giles, London 1892, p. 1382; of Baller, p. 597; and Mathews, p. 1777, all contain the following surprising error: that is that they have incorporated α, β, π(?) of Aries within Chinese constellation No. 9 as well as in Chinese constellations Nos. 16 & 17 where Aries properly belongs.

32 Curiously, the relationship between the constellations and the days of the week have never, so far as I know, been identified. The Dictionaries cited in the previous note (31) speak of associated elements (why seven and why the Sun and the Moon?). But each Agent is also the name of a planet, and the five planets with the addition of the sun and moon are known as the 'seven luminaries', 七曜, *ch'i Yao*. See *Ming Yun Ta Kuan* op. cit. p. 31. These seven luminaries coincide precisely with the names of the Western days of the week. This can hardly be by chance.

33 Quoted by Granet in 'la Pensée Chinoise', p. 177. See also his rather too systematic an explanation ibid. p. 182, et seq.

34 Granet, op. cit., pp. 151, 160–161, 173.

35 All the early translators of the *I Ching* despised divination as a childish superstition. However, since the *I Ching* is the most venerated of the Chinese Classics and the only book to have escaped destruction in the auto da fé of the Emperor 秦始皇 *Ch'in Shih Huang*, these translators thought that it could have nothing to do with divination but must have a hidden meaning.

The premise of this syllogism being false, since, in Chinese eyes, divination is a highly religious and moral act, the translations made by these people were necessarily misleading and therefore useless for our purpose.

R. Wilhelm, in his *I Ching* (English translation by C. F. Baynes, New York 1950) for which Jung wrote an introduction and commentary, was the first translation to have a real understanding of the meaning of the book. Later translators of the *I Ching* have been inspired by Wilhelm's work, with the exception of John Blofeld who has made a fresh translation and, in my opinion, has caught the spirit of the *I Ching* better than anyone else and, at the same time, has penetrated the sybilline style of the Chinese text. See Blofeld, *'I Ching', the Book of Change,* Mandala Books, Unwin Paperbacks, London 1965.

36 Blofeld, op. cit., p. 225, et seq. (for the benefit of the reader I have put in chart form the table referred to).

37 This photo of a very beautiful geomantic compass was given to me by its owner, Mme Gazai-Normandin.

38 These cosmic influences are those described in the *Nei Ching*, ch. 68.

39 The Chinese have used the decimal system from the very beginning. The ideograms of the denary cycle, on which the ten day 'week' was based, are the oldest known and go back to the *Shang* dynasty, 1300 BC. For computing the calendar, the Chinese found the duodecimal system more practical and this appeared a little later. Thereafter the combination of the two systems produced the sexagesimal cycle used to name every measurable part of time: years, months, days and hours. But the denary and duodenary series are also still used separately for series of 10 or 12 things other than time.

40 The terms *Yin* and *Yang* are so often used in books on China that it is not necessary to translate them. Roughly, *Yin* is feminine and receptive while *Yang* is masculine and positive. They are opposite and complementary aspects of everything in nature (see p. 10, et seq., of this book).

41 All the popular works in English or in French on Chinese astrology speak of lunar astrology and pay no attention to the warning given in some Chinese manuals of divination that for a horoscope it is necessary to base the calculation of binomials of the year and the month on the solar terms (see p. 61 of this book) and not on the lunar months.

See the concordance between Chinese and Western calendars 陰陽曆對照百中經, *Yin Yang Li Tui Chao Pei Chung Ching*, which is found in all Chinese almanacks, p. 71; and also the little divinatory manual 命學講義, *Ming Hsüeh Chiang Yi*, 'Commentary on divination', p. 71, which says expressly that the astrological year and thus the first month begins with the first solar term 立春 *Li ch'un*, the 'establishment of Spring' and not on the first day of the first lunar month, 春節 the 'Spring Festival'. Accordingly, each solar month (period) starts at an odd solar term.

42 The concordance (p. 71) between the Universal calendar and the Chinese lunar calendar is based on a work in Chinese and English called *A Sino-Western Calendar for 2000 years*, published in Peking in 1956. Remember that in the second table (p. 68) astrological periods are based on space (30° of the ecliptic) and not, strictly speaking, on time. This is why it is as important for a Chinese to know the exact hour at which each period begins, as it is for a Western astrologer to know the exact hour at which each sign of the Zodiac begins.

43 As I indicated in note 1, in connection with the term 經 *ching*, it seems ridiculous to use a static word, element, for an idea essentially dynamic (see Chapter 4, p. 17 of this book).

44 This table, taken from 命運大觀, *Ming Yün Ta Kuan*, 'Survey of the cycle of Destiny', Hongkong, 1955, Part II, p. 64, is a mnemonic in verses, each of seven feet. The Chinese have thousands of mnemonic verses of this kind which record their oral traditions, on which divination and acupuncture are based. Most of this book, in fact, is based ultimately on such verses. The relationship between the binomials and the Agents is constant. The earliest mention of these relationships that I have been able to find is in 抱朴子, *Pao P'u tzŭ*, 'Book of the preservation-of-solidarity Master', by 葛洪 *Ko Hung* (4th century AD) in *Chu Tzü Chi Ch'eng*, op. cit., Vol. VIII, pp. 51 and 52. See also Needham, op. cit., Vol. V, part 3, p. 75, et seq.

45 The ideogram given here is 劍, *chien*, which means a 'two-edged sword'. However, I prefer the ideogram 釵 *ch'ai*, which means 'hairpin', taken from 命理捷徑, *Ming Li Chieh Ching*, 'Short Guide to the Principles of Divination', Taipei 1969, p. 5.

46 In antiquity, a person born on a given day was given as his name the denary sign of the day. Granet sees in this fact the origin of divination based on the cyclic characters. See M. Granet *La Pensée Chinoise*, Paris 1934, p. 157, and note.

47 This is taken almost word for word from *Nei Ching*, ch. 68.

48 This list is given in *Ming Yün Ta Kuan*, op. cit., part III, pp. 66 and 69. See also *Hsiang Jen Fa* 相人法 'Self Taught Physiognomy', Hong Kong, 1970, pp. 114 and 115.

49 This chart combines in simplified form a number of Chinese charts and represents a synthesis of what we have discussed up to this point. It indicates all the possible relationships between the binomials, cyclic signs and Agents.

50 See *Pao P'u Tzŭ*, op. cit. (note 9) pp. 77 and 78.

51 There are many Western works which base Chinese divination solely on the twelve animals of the year, and sometimes supplemented for good measure by the Western signs of the Zodiac for the month.

Among these books the only one worth noting is *The Handbook of Chinese Horoscopes*, London, 1980, by Theodora *Lau*, a Chinese lady from Shanghai but now living in Hongkong. The author has constructed a more than usually detailed system of divination which, to me, seems unhappily to be based only on the lunar year and also on a confusion between the cyclic signs and the animals. She attributes an animal to the year and also, quite rightly, to the Chinese hour; the latter she describes as the ascendant. Then, somewhat casually, she identifies the animals with the signs of the Zodiac. This does not conform at all with the traditional Chinese concept of the astrological periods (see p. 18 of my book).

The author takes no account of the day, so important in Chinese divination, and this suggests that she is ignorant of the 八字, *pa tzŭ*, eight signs which are the basis of Chinese popular divination (see p. 23 and note 20 of this book).

Her use of the Agents, which she calls 'elements', seems to me to be even more wayward.

Nevertheless this book contains much that is interesting and would have been more so if the author had given her sources.

The drawings of the animals in this chapter are taken from the 相術學, *Hsiang Shu Hsüeh*, 'Studies on Physiognomony' by 張耀文, *Chang Yüeh-wen*, T'ainan, 1975, pp. 34 and 35. Descriptions and interpretations of the character of each are mostly based on *Ming Yün Ta Kuan*, op. cit., part III, p. 6, et seq.

52 The list of the 28 Constellations can be found in Harvet & Chambeau, op. cit.; in Needham, op. cit., vol. III, p. 234; as well as in most of the Chinese-English dictionaries.

53 The illustrations and the accompanying texts are given in all Chinese almanacks.

54 The illustrations and the text of the 'Song of the Four Seasons' come from an ancient book of xylographs reproduced in Hongkong, under the title of 三世相 *San Shih Hsiang*, 'Divination of three Generations', p. 39. An indication, not very clear, suggests that the carving was made in the 53rd year of *Ch'ien Lung*, 1788.

55 The list comes from *Ming Yüng Ta Kuan*, op. cit., part II, p. 65, et seq.

56 ibid. part III, p. 65, et seq.

GLOSSARY

The Chinese have many methods of divination, none of which can truly be called astrology. The eight signs are really numbers and Chinese divination should more accurately be described as numerology. Some terms used in this Glossary (Astrology, Divination, Horoscope) are not strictly applicable to the Chinese context.

ACUPUNCTURE Pricking with a needle. The insertion of needles into living tissues in order to restore the balance of energies in the body, thus preventing or curing diseases.

AFFINITY Favourable conjunction between two or more signs, or between two or more horoscopes; complementarity.

AGENTS (FIVE) The five forces active in the Universe: Wood, Fire, Earth, Metal, Water. We prefer this term to 'element' which is more commonly used by Western authors but which seems to us to be too static.

ANIMALS (TWELVE) Ancient symbols associated within the Duodenary Cycle (q.v.). They must, however, not be identified with these signs nor with the Western signs of the Zodiac. N.B. We have preferred to use Buffalo instead of Ox; Hare instead of Rabbit; Snake instead of Serpent; Goat instead of Sheep; Cock instead of Rooster; Pig instead of Boar; Turtle instead of Tortoise.

ASTROLOGY Practical Astronomy; the application of astronomy to the prediction of events natural and moral. The art of judging the occult influences of the stars upon human affairs. By extension, any kind of divination.

BESTIARY List of animals linked by the Chinese with the points of the compass (capital letters), the Duodenary Signs (q.v.) – (roman numerals), the twenty-eight Constellations (q.v.) – (arabic numerals) Badger, 3; Bat, 10; (Vermilion) Bird, S; Buck, 24; Buffalo, II, 3; Cock, X, 18; Crocodile, 1; Crow, 19; Dog X, 16; Dragon, V, 2; (Green) Dragon, E; Fox, 5; Gibbon, 12; Goat, VIII, 23; Hare, IV, 4; Horse, VII, 25; Leopard, 7; Monkey, IX, 20; Pig, XII, 13; Pheasant, 17; Porcupine, 14; Rat, I, 11; Snake, VI, 27; Stag, 26; Swallow, 12; Tapir, 22; Tiger, III, 6; (White) Tiger, W; (Black) Turtle, N; Unicorn, 8; Wolf, 15; Worms, 28.

BINOMIALS (FOUR) A binomial is composed of two ideograms belonging, first, to the Denary Cycle (q.v.) and, second, to the Duodenary Cycle (q.v.). They define time for the Chinese. The binomials are also known as the 'Pillars' of Destiny (q.v.).

CELESTIAL STEMS The Denary Signs (q.v.).

CONSTELLATIONS (TWENTY-EIGHT) The twenty-eight stations, or lunar dwellings, of the Moon during one revolution around the Earth. Their positions appear to correspond to the ecliptic as it existed 4,400 years ago. As with the signs of the Zodiac, it has been a long time since any of them corresponded to a lunar day.

COSMIC CYCLE Cycle, as defined in the *Nei Ching*, which comprises the 五運, *wu Yun*, 'the five movements', and the 六氣, *liu Ch'i* 'the six energies', linked respectively with Earth and Heaven. The Cosmic Cycle therefore rules all the phenomena of the Universe. It is quite different from the astrological Cycle which rules the destiny of an individual.

CYCLIC CHARACTERS See Signs of Destiny.

DENARY CYCLE Numerical series of ten signs (Cyclic characters) also known as the Celestial Stems.

DIVINATION Method of foretelling future events or discovering those things that are hidden or obscure, often by using pretended magical or supernatural means.

DUODENARY CYCLE Numerical series of twelve signs (Cyclic characters) also known as the Terrestrial Branches.

ECLIPTIC Orbit described by the Earth in the course of a year.

ELEMENTS See Agents.

EMBOLISM Intercalary month used in Greek and Chinese calendars to compensate for the difference between the solar year (astronomical) and the twelve lunar months.

EQUINOX One of the two periods of the year when day and night are of equal length, owing to the Sun crossing the Equator: 20 March and 22 or 23 September. For the Chinese it marks the culminating point and not the beginning of the season. The Spring equinox or point gamma of the ecliptic (q.v.) with the entry of the Sun in the sign of Aries, marks the beginning of the traditional astrological cycle in the West.

GEOMANCY This term is used somewhat differently in this book from the meaning generally given to it in the West (divination by throwing earth on a table and studying the shapes thus made). Chinese geomancy is concerned with defining, with the help of a compass and the cyclic characters (in their relationship with the cardinal points), the most auspicious siting and orientation for a monument, a dwelling or a tomb.

HOROSCOPE An observation of the sky and of the configuration of the planets at a certain moment, e.g. the instant of a person's birth; hence a plan of the planets and the twelve signs of the Zodiac (q.v.) showing the disposition of the heavens at a particular moment.

The Chinese horoscope is based on four constant cycles (sexagesimal q.v.) defining respectively the year, the month, the day and the hour.

HOUR (CHINESE) Equivalent of two Western hours. The first begins at 2300 hours and culminates at midnight; the second begins at 0100 hours and culminates at 0200 hours, etc.

IDEOGRAM A character or figure symbolising the idea of a thing without expressing the name of it, as the Chinese characters, etc.

INTERCALARY Supplementary month or day, like 29 February in a leap year.

LUMINARIES (SEVEN) The Sun, Moon, and the five principal planets: Mars, Mercury, Jupiter, Venus, Saturn. Each luminary appears four times in a period of twenty-eight days, the time taken by the Moon to return to the same point in the ecliptic. The luminaries correspond exactly with the seven days of the week.

LUNAR DWELLINGS See the twenty-eight Constellations.

LUNATION (OR LUNAR MONTH) Duration of the revolution of the Moon around the Earth.

NUMEROLOGY Divination based on figures and numbers.

PERIOD To avoid confusion, we use this term to denote the astrological months which bear the names of the binomials (q.v.). Each describes 30 degrees of the ecliptic but begins 15 degrees before the Western signs of the Zodiac.

PILLARS OF DESTINY (FOUR) The four binomials (q.v.): for the year, the month, the day and the hour which define each moment. Equivalent to the 'Eight Signs' of Destiny.

SEXAGESIMAL CYCLE Cycle of sixty binomials (q.v.), formed by the combination of the Denary and the Duodenary Cycles.

SIGNS OF DESTINY (EIGHT) The ideograms which indicate every moment in time and are the foundation of every horoscope. They come from two series of numbers, the one denary and the other duodenary, called Cyclic Characters. Synonymous with the 'four pillars' of Destiny (q.v.) or four Binomials (q.v.).

SOLAR TERMS (TWENTY-FOUR) Division of the Solar year into twenty-four parts, each corresponding to 15 degrees of the ecliptic. Odd-numbered terms are called, *chieh*, 'joints' or 'divisions'; even-numbered terms are called, *ch'i*, 'energy'. A *chieh* and the following *ch'i* form a period, or astrological month. *Ch'i* terms correspond exactly with the Western signs of the Zodiac, and thus Chinese astrological periods begin about fifteen days before the sign of the Zodiac. Since the winter stations are shorter than the summer ones, it is necessary, as with the signs of the Zodiac, to take account of the precise time at which each period begins.

SOLSTICE One or other of the two times in the year, midway between the two equinoxes (q.v.), when the Sun, having reached the tropical points is farthest from the equator and appears to stand still, i.e. about 21 June and 22 December. For the Chinese, it marks the culmination and not the beginning of the season.

SYMPATHY Reciprocal attraction, the tie of friendship between two signs or between two individuals.

TERRESTRIAL BRANCHES The Duodenary Signs (q.v.).

THEME (ASTROLOGICAL) The assembly of concrete data, the position of the stars at a given moment, on which a horoscope is based. This term, somewhat inexact when Chinese divination is concerned, consists only in finding the four binomials (q.v.) or the Eight Signs (q.v.) and the dominant constellation.

YANG The male or active principle.

YIN The female or receptive principle.

ZODIAC A belt of the celestial sphere extending 8 or 9 degrees at each side of the ecliptic (q.v.), within which the apparent motions of the Sun, Moon and principal planets take place; it is divided into equal parts called signs.

ZODIAC (CHINESE) Improperly applied to the twelve animals (q.v.), for they are not associated with the Constellations of the Western Zodiac, but rather with the numerical series of the Duodenary Signs (q.v.). Correctly used if the twenty-eight Constellations (q.v.), lunar dwellings, in the course of a lunation (q.v.) are meant.